Doomed From Birth

How to Dig Your Way Out of a Hole in Life

Nelson Powell

Dedication

This book is dedicated to my dad, Jesse Powell; my mom, Mary Stills; my brother, Michael Stills; my sister, Christina Stills; my grandmother, Hattie Stills; and my three sons, Isaiah, Joshua, and Elijah. I would also like to dedicate special dedication to Jennifer Bicknell, an inspiration in my life and my future wife.

Acknowledgment

Writing "Doomed From Birth" has been an incredible journey filled with introspection, challenges, and hope. Along this path, I've been fortunate to receive support, guidance, and inspiration from many remarkable individuals, without whom this book would not have been possible.

First and foremost, I extend my deepest gratitude to the love of my life, Jennifer, whose unwavering love and encouragement have been my rock throughout this endeavor. Your belief in me has been the driving force.

I am indebted to my editor and the publishing team for their expertise, patience, and dedication in helping shape this manuscript into its final form.

Lastly, to the readers of "Doomed From Birth," thank you for embarking on this journey with me. May the pages of this book serve as a reminder that no matter how dire our circumstances may seem, we always possess the power to choose our path forward.

With heartfelt thanks,

Nelson Powell

About the Author

Nelson Powell is the Principal and CEO of Night Owl Investors LLC—a privately held, fully integrated residential and commercial real estate investment firm based in Trenton, New Jersey. The company primarily acquires, renovates, and repositions class C and D residential and commercial properties. Mr. Powell started as an apartment cleaner in 1995. He then worked his way as a maintenance technician from 1996-2004. From there, Mr. Powell purchased a 24-unit building and started a home renovation company where he managed ten employees. He has played significant roles as a project manager to help grow a few real estate investment companies from the ground up. Over the years, he has also been a part of acquiring great cash-producing assets. Over the last 20 years, Mr. Powell has had hands-on experience in every part of the real estate industry.

As a principal, he identifies opportunistic real estate investments that will create yield. He oversees all negotiations, construction, payroll, acquisitions, team building, investor relations, company growth, and leasing activity. Mr. Powell has been with the Night Owl Investors team since 2017.

Mr. Powell volunteered for eight years as the Athletic Director at the Trenton Boys & Girls Club. During this time, he started a youth basketball league and coached an AAU program that traveled nationwide. Mr. Powell also volunteered and coached at Trenton Central High School for four years.

Contents

Introduction

In this book, *Doomed From Birth*, I am trying to shed light on a serious problem that should concern America but has been completely neglected. It's implausible that children and adults are still living in extreme poverty to this day and in the so-called modern age.

Generation after generation, the cycle of poverty continues to overshadow the futures of young children and adults alike. These children don't have a say in where they are born and the environment in which they are raised.

It is certainly not fair to them. Being raised around negativity breeds more negativity, which is all they're familiar with.

Where do these young children go from there?

I can imagine they can't envision a future that doesn't look like the present. All they know and have seen is poverty, drugs, gangs, guns, stabbings, welfare, rats, crime, murder, hunger, deprivation of electricity and heat, Section 8 housing, project housing, jail, absence of a father, trash, graffiti, drug dealers, prostitution, alcohol abuse, foul language, police raids, ambulance sirens, and buildings boarded up everywhere.

You learn to get used to the misery of everything around you as a kid, but that shouldn't mean it dictates the course of your life, especially the future. It shouldn't mean that you are doomed.

At some point, you must look at yourself and scream, "This is not my life!"

Once you say that out loud, you will start thinking of ways to get rid of the rotten life; once you have made up your mind to pursue a better life for yourself, you have to know and understand that it will not be easy.

Climbing your way out of a hole this deep will take all the effort, drive, faith, and belief you can muster every day despite the lack of a better outcome.

You must find a way to entirely focus on making your dream happen. If you read this book and find a way to pull it off, you will have a better life, and your present or future children will also have a better life.

I intend to help you learn some ways to work your way out of your current situation and see real hope for your future and future generations with this book.

Chapter 1: The Beginning

Wealthy and well-to-do people live and die every day. They spend their lives focused on themselves, family, friends, and business as they should. They remain clueless about an entire world out there - a world doomed from birth. A world that has been going through a cycle of poverty that seems never to end. A world where children are being born but have a very slim chance of survival.

It's the world I grew up in. It's a dog-eat-dog world for survival. It was a neighborhood of mostly crack addicts, prostitutes, and drug dealers. Don't get me wrong. Some good people in the hood loved the street or neighborhood so much that they didn't want to leave. These people chose to be held hostage. And they find a way to block all the noise and negativity out.

My first memory goes back to when I was three or four. We lived in an abandoned house on an abandoned street in New Jersey. I remember walking around the house without any clothes except a diaper.

I can recall a poverty-stricken household. The furniture looked old and worn out. The floors and walls also looked like they were old. The house had a smell like an old abandoned house. For some reason, this was my home, and my parents thought it was where we should set up camp. I was young and had no say in deciding where we should live.

I think it was where the cycle began for precious, intelligent, and talented young children who are doomed from birth. They are condemned to a life of constant struggle for survival and dealing with pain that was never their fault to begin with.

When you are born to parents who only know the streets and are only familiar with survival in such a dangerous environment, they will naturally teach you those survival skills since that is all they know to survive. Their parents only knew how to survive, and so did the ones before them.

Growing up in this type of household, let's start with how my parents talked. They talked in slang, which is considered an uneducated form of English. Our neighbors, friends, and family mostly understood it. That was how everyone around me communicated.

Along with the slang comes all the curse words, as foul language is vital to communication. Hearing this language day in and day out, I learned to speak it very well. Remember, this was going on inside the home.

Now, here I am, the third generation of survivors. I had no idea what awaited me once I walked out the door. I remember seeing broken glass and trash everywhere. There were a lot of dirty-looking people just standing around street corners and many bums and drunks lying in the streets.

I saw that the other houses looked just like mine. They were also boarded up. This was all a part of my life, and I had not even turned ten. It was at this age that things went from bad to worse.

My mom got addicted to crack cocaine. But it wasn't just her; almost every adult I knew was on crack. I even saw my school teachers in my neighborhood buying crack.

Everyone around me was either on drugs or selling them to others. I will never forget my cousin Jesse, an honor roll student in 5th grade who said he wanted to be the President of the United States, and yet he had started selling crack by the time he reached eighth grade.

It was a real turning point in my life. It was when I felt that I was on my own. If I couldn't rely on the adults closest to me, I had to rely on myself to find a way to the life I wanted.

Crack hit my neighborhood like a nuclear bomb. Whatever was left of the family structure was destroyed. It became a dog-eat-dog kind of environment. All of us were stuck in a fishbowl, trying to survive through all this insanity.

You could see the life you wanted through the glass, but the glass was so high that you couldn't climb out. Living in this type of environment could turn a lot of people into animals, and when you turn into an animal, the government says you should be physically locked in a cage.

Imagine millions of children nationwide growing up in this environment. The percentage of them finding a way to climb out of this hole is slim to none.

This could drive someone crazy. But with the right plan and mindset, it is very possible.

The question is when this cycle changes.

When does poverty end?

Chapter 2: Generational Cycle

My family's financial deprivations didn't start with my parents. My grandparents' life wasn't very different from the one my parents had. They were forced to live in poverty, which limited their access to many fundamental necessities.

My grandparents' generation didn't have the amenities that mine does. If you were born poor in their time, you were supposed to make the best you could while living a life of poverty.

My grandparents didn't have much scope regarding working toward a future that could bring them financial stability. Things that were essential to their lives weren't accessible, and they struggled to make ends meet.

Ironically, life is filled with opportunities and options when one has the capital to afford them. Yet, without financial stability, it's hard to find the means to better yourself, which could improve your quality of life.

My grandparents were undoubtedly aware of their social class and what they should expect out of life.

These were the hands that life had dealt them: having children and struggling to give them what they deserved was not what they would have chosen for themselves.

Like every other parent, they also yearned to provide their kids with a life free from obstacles every step of the way. They wanted their children to have a better life than them, but they still faced the challenge of poverty.

Owing to their financial condition, they had to stay in a neighborhood they could afford. They couldn't live anywhere else as their pockets didn't allow them. They had to make the best out of whatever resources they had.

My grandparents faced more challenges as their children started growing up. They needed food in their stomach, clothes, books for school, and a roof over their head.

There was only so much that could be done. My grandparents worked hard to provide a good life for their kids. Of course, their financial backgrounds limited them to certain professions, and they couldn't move beyond the social conditioning, but they were determined to carve a path to a better life. They didn't want their children running in the streets. They wanted them to have a secure future.

As they coped with a life of financial deprivation, they developed important insights about surviving poverty. My grandparents were smart people. Anyone in their position could have easily given up, but they didn't.

My grandparents worked their way to the top. They didn't believe in losing hope. They knew their living conditions were deplorable, but they knew that things wouldn't change if they didn't try to change them.

Survival was all my parents and grandparents knew. They might not have had access to the basic facilities everyone deserves, but they had the wisdom they earned through decades of struggle.

My grandparents had learned very early in life that it's not about what you have but what you decide to do with what you have. They made calculated decisions since they couldn't afford to lose their limited capital.

They had to choose some necessities over others. It wasn't much of a choice for them and more of an inevitable decision.

They couldn't manage to provide their children with everything they wanted. My parents saw what other kids had, leaving them feeling deprived. Unfortunately, my grandparents couldn't afford it for them.

My parents witnessed the comfort that other people had in their houses, but they didn't. It was a heart-breaking experience for them to realize they didn't even have access to necessities.

My grandparents realized they needed to build their bond with their children if they needed them to understand what was good or bad for them. They wanted to empower them instead of making them realize where they belonged. They knew that their children had the potential to make it far in their lives if they made the right decisions.Of course, seeing how financially stable people lived wasn't easy. They had nice furniture, a house, a school, and everything they could wish for when they struggled to access the most basic facilities.

Yes, my grandparents never intended to join the herd and follow other people's lead. They decided to carve their path.

Ethics and honesty were the virtues my grandparents valued. They taught us how to focus if we wanted to move forward. We couldn't afford to let ourselves get distracted.

When you live in an environment where you have access to everything that might seem enticing but could also ruin your life, the decisions become problematic. Since you're already coping with a life of difficulties, it's easy to get drawn to activities that might provide you with some moments of relief. This is exactly where everything goes wrong, and my grandparents were aware of this and did their best to prevent it.

They made sure that we believed in ourselves before anyone else. It was easy to let someone else take the steering wheel of our lives, but my grandparents urged us to stand our ground and stick to our beliefs instead of relying on others.

Chapter 3: Changing the Cycle

As humans, we have the power to assume that our individuality and traits inherently belong to us, and we are the ones who have created our personality. However, if we were to retrace our steps and observe closely, we would find that every single one of our traits is linked to someone in our lives.

For instance, a child who witnesses tenderness and composure in his home develops similar traits. They will treat people like they see others treated in their own house. A lack of empathy and consideration will only cause disbelief in the child, and they won't be able to gauge the reason behind someone's lack of kindness.

These traits are developed during childhood and only grow stronger as the child grows up. They will find that they have created a certain perspective on life and see the world through the lens they have evolved over the years, watching people around them.

On the contrary, a child who grows up witnessing rigid and toxic tendencies in their house will only take after the people they have been interacting with. They will try to express themself. Or, worse, take out their frustration on other people who are not their family.

After a while, these traits will become so firm and deep-rooted that they will find it hard to understand why their actions aren't helping them or any others around them. They have adapted to the environment they have witnessed and expect the same treatment for other people.

These traits or learned behaviors carry on for decades and get passed on to the next generation, known as a lifecycle. We don't realize we are all part of a chain and serve as agents who transfer traits to the next generation.

Whatever we do at any moment might not seem like it will affect anyone in the future as we assume that our actions are limited to ourselves. But the crucial fact remains that anything you put out there returns to you and the people around you.

We must understand that our actions and learned behavior can develop into patterns. Something that might not seem like a big deal will eventually yield more considerable consequences and form a chain of learned behavior.

We assume these traits can be washed away with time and get milder, but sadly, that's not the case. Characteristics inherited from the previous generation grow their roots within us and develop in an environment that will sustain those characteristics.

Inherited traits are transferred to the next generation, and we don't have a choice. Your mind adapts the survival skills necessary to navigate your life and eventually decides that those traits will assist the ones you procreate, unintentionally making the characteristics part of your life.

People don't realize this, but we have the power to alter our characteristics and traits if we're willing to do so. The most significant factor affecting an individual's personality is the social condition surrounding them.

We naturally adapt to the external environment we live in. If we find ourselves in a social situation that doesn't align with our personality, we try to mold ourselves into a more agreeable form.

It isn't easy to alter an individual's perspective, but how they act around certain people can change depending on their social conditioning.

Remember that humans don't build their personalities and traits by themselves. We are nothing but the reflection of our surroundings. Social and cultural norms are a factor in our lives and significantly alter how we see the world.

These norms and conditions have the power to consume an individual with their structure, eventually leading that individual to accept the situation and try to make themselves acceptable to fit in.

Think about someone belonging to a family that has a below-average income and is used to limit access to a facilitated lifestyle. They will act according to what they have learned from their surroundings. Their financial, professional, and personal decisions will heavily rely on their understanding of a world learned from their previous generation.

When the same individual gets exposed to a drastically different environment where they are supposed to interact with people with a financially secure background, they will start to notice a change in their behavior.

The change due to social and cultural exposure is known as acquired traits. These are not the traits someone is born with. They witness these characteristics and figure out how they benefit their personal growth.

Soon, the individual will start making the necessary changes to sustain the expected lifestyle. The inherited traits will remain with them, but they will take a back seat while they adjust to social conditioning.

, They will also go through a phase where they must choose between sticking to the notions they had acquired earlier while growing up in a specific environment and adapting to the newfound social condition.

Ultimately, individuals will choose the traits that benefit them and will help them grow. It's not a conscious choice, but it's inevitable. They will have to adapt to survive and progress while they're at it.

Yes, the life cycle isn't something that can change overnight. We have learned and practiced survival skills needed to live a comfortable life. But we must realize that that sense of comfort stops us from expanding our horizons and exploring a life we could have.

The first step in breaking a life cycle that doesn't benefit us is distancing ourselves from the surroundings that force us to maintain the same lifestyle that hasn't been helping us grow.

Moving away from your comfort zone takes a lot of courage, but it's not impossible.

We must understand that we cannot prosper in the same unhealthy situation that keeps us from living a better life. No matter how much we believe that we have control over life, in the end, it's the objective environment around us that influences our decisions.

Someone needs to step in to break a life cycle. It might happen once in four generations, but it's bound to happen. We have to recognize what we lack in our lives and how we can make up for the absence by trying to accommodate the necessary changes.

At one point, we will need to look at ourselves and observe which inherited traits add to our lives and which are holding us back. Once we have identified the characteristics we have been carrying that aren't benefitting us, we will have to decide to get rid of them gradually.

Of course, the life cycle that has been carried on for generations won't end that easily. The process will take time, and we need to be patient. We can't rush into altering the course of our lives as we might make a rash decision that won't help us in the end.

The next challenge that you will come across during the process of changing a life cycle would be the tendency to retreat. You might find that the new lifestyle you're creating for yourself might not provide you the same satisfaction you expected.

We need to understand that people are creatures of habits, and despite wanting to make a long-term change, we might find that we have the urge to return to the same old life since it provides us with the comfort and ease we crave. It's the point where the process becomes tricky.

If we want to continue progressing, we must firmly intend to move forward no matter what. Comfort can be extremely enticing, making you want to retrace your steps, but you will only end up with the same life cycle that your previous generations have been a part of.

Eventually, we must prioritize ourselves and the person we want to be. Life will only keep dragging you along, and you will have to deal with mishaps if you don't control your fate. We must change our perspective and make the necessary changes that will help us grow and prosper in our lives.

Chapter 4: Change Your Mindset

We often fail to recognize the extent to which our brain controls how we behave.

Our actions are influenced by our thoughts, feelings, beliefs, and habits. If you want to alter your life, you must first change your mindset.

HOW YOUR MIND WORKS?

Our ideas and emotions have a profound influence on both our reality and the reality of those around us. However, many people find it challenging to grasp this idea, let alone apply it in real life.

How are we ever going to escape what makes us who we are?

How can we alter something that has always existed?

We must know what we are thinking about when selecting from various possibilities. We must develop control of our minds if we want to live a happy life.

At first, you might not understand how much power your thoughts and feelings have on your day-to-day activities. They influence every part of our daily lives, even the ones we aren't actively aware of.THE POWER OF THE MIND: WHAT YOU THINK ABOUT IS WHO YOU ARE

When you wake up every morning, you have a set of preconceived notions, subconscious and assumptions, that make up who you are and influence your identity.

These ideas are established due to prior events and repeatedly reinforced throughout your lifetime. For example, "I am worthless" or "I am terrible at math." These are negative thoughts and ideas you have about yourself due to the state of your mindset.

You need to start changing your point of view to make progress toward a happier state of being.

THOUGHTS HAVE THE POWER TO AFFECT HOW YOU FEEL AND LIVE.

In this chapter, we'll examine some of the most prevalent limiting notions and negative self-talk habits to enable you to start changing your life. I will also show you some basic ways to permanently eliminate these negative thought patterns.

You'll start to form new, empowering beliefs as you go through them one at a time. You'll be able to create a better future as a result.

THE CONSCIOUS MIND

The thoughts you decide to focus on are called the conscious mind. That is, the things you choose to participate in. As a result, your conscious thinking often differs from your subconscious mind.

For instance, if you are considering a promotion but your subconscious mind understands you aren't likely to land the position because there aren't sufficient funds in your budget, your conscious mind will be aware that you weren't planning to buy the new car. Yet, your subconscious will still decide to purchase it.

So, it's simple to see why strengthening your conscious mind is essential. Your life will have greater meaning and purpose if you are mindful of your choices and act accordingly.

THE UNCONSCIOUS MIND

Every day of the week, your subconscious mind is running programs.

It records your countless ideas, sights, sounds, and experiences throughout each waking second of your life.

It consequently records all of this data in the recesses of your brain. It creates associations, anticipations, judgments, responses, routines, and beliefs that shape your personality there.

When the subconscious receives powerful signals from the conscious mind, it can overpower doubts or worries. This explains why so many people struggle to release their old habits. You need ongoing drive, perseverance, and awareness to continue moving forward despite those unfavorable signals ringing in your thoughts.

WHY YOU NEED TO CONTROL YOUR MIND INSTEAD OF LETTING IT CONTROL YOU

How often have you considered giving up on a particular individual or habit because it emotionally damaged you? Or perhaps you've recently experienced a failed relationship and are now wondering why it didn't work out.

Humans frequently depend on their feelings. However, these emotional responses occasionally prevent us from accomplishing our objectives. We should attempt to regulate our emotions rather than allow them to rule us.

You must have emotional self-control if you want to succeed. To achieve this, you must learn to regulate your emotions rather than letting them rule you.

WHY YOU SHOULD DOMINATE YOUR THOUGHTS RATHER THAN LETTING THEM DOMINATE YOU

Though having negative thoughts is not something you can develop a habit of, there are techniques to alter the patterns that have developed in your mind.

Try to break the habit of thinking negative or demeaning ideas when you discover yourself doing so by replacing them with upbeat ones (or, if none naturally occur to you, pick one and hold onto it).

We eventually educate our brains to identify the type of idea approaching and swiftly replace it. This procedure significantly enhances our mental health when we consistently practice it.

It is crucial to begin educating ourselves as soon as possible since the more frequently we think negatively, the simpler it is to fall into this thinking.

HOW TO CHANGE YOUR MINDSET

Your thoughts have a significant impact on the standard of your life. You can guide your life in a way that makes you happy and fulfilled if you have the correct perspective and attitude. Here are fifteen tested tactics that will help you on your journey.

1. PRACTICE GRATITUDE

A positive mindset is built on gratitude. By valuing what you already have, you may turn your attention away from what's lacking in your life and toward what's plentiful.

Start by appreciating your blessings: Spend a few moments daily listing what you are grateful for. It might be as straightforward as having a hearty meal or a bright sunny day.

Try to view difficulties as chances for improvement: Rather than whining about the gridlock, be grateful for the extra time you have to listen to an audiobook.

Show gratitude to others: Whether it's a brief appreciation to a coworker or a sincere card to a loved one, expressing gratitude can make you and the person you're thanking feel happier.

2. CULTIVATE A GROWTH MINDSET

The idea of a development mindset, made famous by psychologist Carol Dweck, can radically alter how you respond to difficulties and failures.

Have faith in your capacity for growth and learning: Instead of "I'm not good at this," say "I'm not good at this yet."

Take mistakes as a learning curve: Remember that being imperfect is okay. What matters most is that you continue to improve.

Celebrate your efforts, not just the results: Did you go to the gym for an extra hour this week? That achievement warrants celebrating!

3. PRACTICE MINDFULNESS

By practicing mindfulness, you can stay grounded in the now and experience less anxiety over the past or future.

Regularly meditate: A few minutes daily might positively impact your mental health.

Take one step at a time. If you're walking, walk. If you're working, work. Put all of your focus on the experience.

Engage in mindful breathing during the day: It can help you calm down and refresh your mind.

4. FOSTER POSITIVE RELATIONSHIPS

Positive influences can significantly impact your mood and frame of mind.

Find people who uplift you and make you feel confident in yourself.

Keep negativity at a distance: It's not always straightforward, but it is crucial for mental health.

Cultivate your relationships: Give time and effort in strengthening bonds with those you care about.

5. ENGAGE IN REGULAR PHYSICAL ACTIVITY

Physical exercise benefits your body as well as your intellect.

Find a workout you like to do: Pilates, tap dancing, trekking, or any other exercise that keeps you moving will do the trick.

Strive for regularity over intensity: A quick walk, even once a day, is preferable to a strenuous workout once a month.

Pay attention to your body: Make an effort, but remember to take time to rest and recover.

6. ADOPT A BALANCED DIET

How you feel is impacted by what you eat. You may improve how you think and how energetic you are by feeding your body nutritious foods.

Put whole foods first. Eat a diet rich in whole grains, lean proteins, fruits, and vegetables.

Reduce your intake of processed foods: They often contain excessive sugar and bad fats that can harm your physical and mental health. Have fun eating. Enjoy every mouthful and be grateful for the nutrients it offers. This might assist you in developing a healthy relationship with food.

7. PRACTICE SELF-CARE

To practice self-care, you must look after your mental, emotional, and physical health. It's about being kind and compassionate to yourself.

Create a schedule that includes the things you enjoy doing. Reading, gardening, art, or any other activity that makes you happy counts.

Give relaxation and sleep a priority. Don't forget to get enough rest and take breaks as needed.

Learn to say no: Don't hesitate to set boundaries to avoid burnout.

8. SET GOALS AND VISUALIZE SUCCESS

Setting objectives can give you a sense of purpose and direction. You can increase your motivation and self-confidence by visualizing achievement.

Establish SMART (specific: measurable, achievable, relevant, and time-bound) objectives. You may be able to keep motivated and focused by doing this.

Envision yourself succeeding: Consider reaching your objectives in as much detail as possible. Feel the pride and enthusiasm.

Celebrate minor accomplishments. Each thing you do that gets you closer to your objective is an accomplishment. Celebrate it!

9. EMBRACE CHANGE

Life is full of change. You may adjust more readily and transform obstacles into opportunities by accepting them.

Recognize change as a chance for growth: Although uncomfortable, change frequently results in personal and professional advancement.

Be adaptable. Be flexible and receptive to fresh ideas.

Learn from change: Each change has a lesson to teach you that can accelerate your development.

10. DEVELOP EMOTIONAL INTELLIGENCE

It takes emotional intelligence to recognize and control your emotions. Your relationships and general well-being can both benefit from it.

Practice self-awareness: Recognize and comprehend your emotions and their influence on thinking and acting.

Effectively manage your emotions: It's acceptable to feel, but don't let your feelings dominate your actions.

Show sympathy for others. Understanding other people's emotions can improve your relationships and interactions with others.

11. NURTURE YOUR CURIOSITY

Curiosity can result in growth and learning. You may find it stimulating and inspiring.

Pose questions: Don't be scared to admit it when you don't know anything.

Seek out new experiences: They can help you get a broader perspective and a more profound comprehension of the world.

Keep an open mind: Be open to fresh perspectives and ideas.

12. SEEK CONTINUOUS LEARNING

The search for knowledge can improve your life and aid in your growth.

Make learning a habit for life: There are numerous ways to know, including through books, online courses, and workshops.

Take advice from people you trust. Every person has something to teach you.

Accept the unknown: It's an opportunity to discover and investigate.

13. PRACTICE RESILIENCE

Being resilient means having the capacity to overcome challenges. You can use it to handle the ups and downs of life.

Maintain an optimistic attitude: Have faith in your abilities to overcome obstacles.

Develop strong relationships: They might be of assistance at difficult times.

Create coping mechanisms: They may include writing in a journal, practicing meditation, or speaking with a friend.

14. CULTIVATE SELF-CONFIDENCE

Possessing self-confidence allows you to pursue your goals and get beyond challenges.

Celebrate your skills: Recognize your strengths and be proud of them.

Learn from your missteps: They are not indications of failure but stepping stones to success.

Practice self-compassion: Be kind to yourself. Keep in mind that nobody is perfect.

15. DEVELOP POSITIVE SELF-TALK

Your thinking and attitude can be influenced by how you speak.

Positive affirmations should be used instead of negative self-talk: Say "I can do it" rather than "I can't."

Embrace self-compassion: Start by reminding yourself that you are trying your best and that making errors is okay.

Celebrate your accomplishments: Acknowledge your growth and achievements regularly.

It takes time to adjust your attitude and frame of mind. It calls for persistent practice and effort. With these fifteen techniques, however, you can start down a path of personal development and change that can result in a healthier and more rewarding life.

Never forget that you have the power to change. You are capable of designing a life that you cherish.[1]

---

[1] https://www.mentalhealthcenter.org/ways-to-change-your-mindset-and-attitude/

Chapter 5: The Plan

I wonder if you've felt like you're drifting steadily away from your desired life with each day that has gone by.

You know there's something more significant out there for you, but you've found it quite difficult to pinpoint it. And trying to make sense of it all by venturing into the unknown might be daunting.

However, what if there was a way to discover your life's purpose with absolute clarity?

Imagine being able to establish a genuine connection with your calling. I think that every person is endowed with incredible talents and passions. And for many, these interests and skills are just waiting to be set free.

Sadly, there are times of difficulty in life, and it's far easier said than done compared to living through them. You find it difficult to manage all the obligations of being a person chasing their dreams.

Perhaps you are among those who are disengaged from their work, fearing for your future, and giving up on ever leading the life you have always imagined.If this describes you, you're most likely leading the life that someone else intended for you to lead.

It's hardly surprising that one of the top five regrets expressed by people on their deathbed is:

"I wish I'd had the courage to live a life true to myself, not the life others expected of me."

Every day, we encounter perspectives on how we should spend our lives, whether from our parents setting expectations for us, the American Dream offering a recipe for "success," or society as a whole.

Things gradually fall into place when we start to live our lives doing what we were uniquely destined for.

This is the critical bit, though.

There is No One-Size-Fits-All Approach to Figuring Out Your True Purpose in Life.

And for this reason—because they were initially searching for the wrong things—people who attempt to find their calling eventually give up.

People want a foolproof plan with all the predetermined solutions, but that's not how your calling works.

For this reason, it is simpler to adhere to formulas like the American Dream to obtain good grades, admission to prestigious universities, and employment.

Having your life all planned out can be comforting, but when that job finally comes around, and you realize this isn't what you want to do with your life, you will have a rude awakening.

And now for the unpalatable truth:

Living the life that another person wants you to live is considerably easier. Therefore, you have probably not taken as much action as you should to fulfill your true calling.

My biggest realization was that, even though I lived according to other people's rules, I never found my calling and followed through because I was terrified to do so.

Dreaming Of a Wonderful Life Is Easier Than Putting in The Effort Necessary to Make It a Reality.

The most unsettling part is that you have no one to hold accountable if something goes wrong once you accept responsibility for the one life you have. You can at least hold someone else responsible if you follow their directions.

Here are three key points to remember about what your calling is and isn't to assist you in discovering your unique position in the world.

1.   Your Calling is Not a Formula

We want to be prepared to quickly determine how to thrive in a world where social media feeds are overrun with how-to guides and schemes to get rich, explaining why, despite trying numerous solutions, most individuals still feel stuck.

You won't start to sense what you are meant to do with your life until you discover who you are and what matters to you. And there is no exact formula for finding your calling. It's more like a compass.

Your Calling Is More Analogous to a Firm Course You Need to Take in Life.

It involves trusting that life is far more than simply you and bravely facing the uncertainty.

And once you acknowledge this, you'll be moving on the right path that ultimately gives your life a profound feeling of purpose—something we're all after.

"Life is never made unbearable by circumstances, but only by lack of meaning and purpose." — Viktor Frankl.

2.   Your Calling Isn't Meant to Give You a Sense of Safety and Security

You have likely experienced this at some point in your life.

Some of you recognize that your best life is waiting for you on the other side, but your worries prevent you from taking advantage of this calling to pursue a different path. It takes courage to venture into the unknown and realize your potential to fulfill your calling. Franklin D. Roosevelt, in my opinion, was right when he said:

"Courage is not the absence of fear but rather the assessment that something else is more important than fear."

Your calling never asks you to give up; it always calls you to keep going. You will discover the confidence to make the necessary big decisions once following your calling takes precedence over your worries.

3.   Your Calling Isn't Always About What You Are Doing, but it Has Everything to do With Who You Are Becoming.

It's true that life is difficult and that some of us have to live in survival mode for the majority of our lives to pay our bills and put food on the table, but making the most of your passions and abilities is the most incredible way to live the one life you have.

We can never become who we were intended to be if we suppress our goals because we are too busy to pursue them.

Every person possesses a deep-seated desire and a distinct set of abilities that can contribute to making a significant difference in the world. Still, we will never discover our actual purpose until we make the time to connect deeply with and develop these qualities.

How to Find Your Unique Calling—Your True Purpose in Life

It's not just a cliché to find your life's purpose; doing so can give you a feeling of direction, fulfillment, and overall contentment. One of the most essential factors in having a happy life is probably feeling that your work is valuable. However, each person's interpretation of this varies.

A New York Times analysis found that only around 25% of Americans clearly know what makes their life meaningful. Another forty percent either say they don't or claim to be neutral.[2]

---

[2] Khullar D. Finding Purpose for a Good Life. But Also a Healthy One. The New York Times. The Upshot. Jan. 1, 2018:1.
https://www.nytimes.com/2018/01/01/upshot/finding-purpose-for-a-good-life-but-also-a-healthy-one.html

Why Do You Need a Sense of Purpose?

According to a 2010 study published in Applied Psychology[3], those with high levels of eudemonic well-being—a sense of control, purpose, and worth in their work—live longer on average. According to findings by other studies[4], well-being may be protective for maintaining health. The strongest well-being participants in the study had a 30% lower death rate throughout the eight-and-a-half-year follow-up period.

Additionally, studies have shown a connection between having a sense of purpose in life and favorable health outcomes[5] like fewer heart attacks and strokes, improved sleep, and a decreased chance of dementia and other disorders.

The good news is that you don't have to give up on leading a fulfilling life in favor of wealth. You may discover that your income increases with your sense of purpose.

Given all those advantages, finding meaning and purpose is essential to fulfillment, but it may take some time and patience.

Finding your passions, reflecting on yourself, and listening to others are necessary.[6] These seven tactics can assist you in

---

[3] Kobau, R, Sniezek, J, Zack, M M, Lucas, RE, Burns, A. Well-Being Assessment: An Evaluation of Well-Being Scales for Public Health and Population Estimates of Well-Being among US Adults. Applied Psychology: 2010: 2: 272-297. doi.org/10.1111/j.1758-0854.2010.01035.x

[4] Steptoe A, Deaton A, Stone AA. Subjective wellbeing, health, and ageing. Lancet. 2015;385(9968):640–648. doi:10.1016/S0140-6736(13)61489-0

[5] Musich S, Wang SS, Kraemer S, Hawkins K, Wicker E. Purpose in Life and Positive Health Outcomes Among Older Adults. Popul Health Manag. 2018;21(2):139–147. doi:10.1089/pop.2017.0063

[6] Schippers MC, Ziegler N. Life Crafting as a Way to Find Purpose and Meaning in Life. Front Psychol. 2019;10:2778. doi: 10.3389/fpsyg.2019.02778

discovering or revealing your purpose and start living a more purposeful life:

Donate Time, Money, or Talent

If you could only establish one useful behavior in your quest for meaning, it would be to help others.

Happiness and meaningfulness, according to researchers at Florida State University and Stanford, overlapped yet differed: Meaningfulness was associated with being more of a giver than a taker, but happiness was associated with being a taker before being a giver. In relationships, givers claimed to lead meaningful lives more frequently than takers.[7]

Volunteering for a charitable organization, making financial contributions to groups you support, or lending a hand to those in your community are examples of philanthropic actions.[8]

Doing good deeds for others can give you a sense of purpose in life, whether you volunteer to drive an elderly neighbor to the supermarket once a week or spend two Saturdays every month serving meals in a soup kitchen.

Listen to Feedback

Sometimes, it's challenging to identify the things you're enthusiastic about. Ultimately, you likely have a wide range of

---

[7] Baumeister RF, Vohs KD, Aaker JL, Garbinsky EN. Some key differences between a happy life and a meaningful life. The Journal of Positive Psychology. 2013;8(6):505-516. doi:10.1080/17439760.2013.830764

[8] Son J. Wilson J. Volunteer Work and Hedonic, Eudemonic, and Social Well-Being. Sociological Forum. 2012;27(3):658-681. doi:10.1111/j.1573-7861.2012.01340.x

interests, and the activities you enjoy may have grown so engrained in your life that you are unaware of their significance.

Thankfully, there may be those who can shed some light on the situation. You probably already show people around you your passion and purpose without realizing it.

You could decide to make contact with folks and find out what comes to mind when they think of you or what reminds them of you. On the other hand, you could keep track of the compliments you receive or the observations made about you. Take notes on your observations and search for trends.

Hearing what others say about you, whether they call you "a great entertainer" or "you have a passion for helping the elderly," may reaffirm some of your passions.

Surround Yourself with Positive People

You are the company you keep, as they say. What qualities do the individuals you choose to surround yourself with have in common with you?

Put your obligations to see family members or coworkers out of your mind. Consider who you hang out with when you're not working or attending family events. The people you choose to surround yourself with have an impact on you. You may find inspiration in those around you who bring about positive change.

However, you may want to make specific changes if the people in your life are bringing you down or are negative people. Being surrounded by people who don't want to make a positive difference makes it difficult to feel passionate and purposeful.

Start Conversations with New People

Sitting at a bar waiting for a friend or alone on the subway makes it effortless to scroll through social media. Defy that impulse. Spend time conversing with those in your immediate vicinity instead.

Find out what they enjoy doing for leisure or if they are working on any projects. Ask them about the groups they participate in or whether they have a favorite cause for donations.

Talking to people outside of your social circle can open your eyes to hobbies, causes, or job opportunities that you never even knew existed, even though discussing with a stranger may feel odd initially.

You might come across fresh pursuits or new locations to see. Such pursuits may be crucial in helping you discover your calling.

Explore Your Interests

Do you often talk about a subject in tweets or Facebook status updates? Do you regularly share stories on refugees or climate change?

Do you have any Instagram photos of you repeatedly doing something, like gardening or performing?

Think about the discussions you love having in-person meetings with people the most. Do you enjoy discussing the past? Or would you instead share the newest money-saving advice you come across?

Your purpose in life may be revealed through the topics you enjoy discussing and posting about on social media.

Consider Injustices That Bother You

Many people are passionate about causes or projects that address injustices worldwide. Is there something that profoundly disturbs you and makes you feel miserable?

It might be organizations that fight childhood obesity, a specific civil rights problem, or animal welfare. Maybe you feel that there should be more options for substance abusers to receive rehabilitation—there are organizations out there that need your support—or you find it heartbreaking to think about older adults spending the holidays alone.

You don't need to devote all of your time to your cause. Your profession may enable you to support a cause you are deeply committed to financially. Alternatively, you may discover you can help a cause you care about by giving time rather than money.

Discover What You Love to Do

Conversely, considering what you genuinely enjoy doing can also assist you in discovering your purpose.

Do you have a deep passion for musical theater? Your talents might be most helpful if they are applied to bringing live performances to kids who could use the exposure to the arts.

Is data analysis something you enjoy doing? That kind of ability might be beneficial to a lot of different groups.

Think about the abilities, interests, and passions you possess. Next, consider how you may make your passion into something of personal significance.

How Do You Know You've Found Your Purpose?

The answer to that is subjective, just like the idea of purpose itself, and there are as many indications that someone has discovered their purpose as there are individuals.

Maybe you have a deep sense of unity with the universe and clearly understand your role. Perhaps religion is where you've discovered significance in life. Or you feel that you have a deep bond with other people. Volunteering and other charitable endeavors may be the source of the emotion.

If you have finally stopped wondering if you have found your calling, you have probably discovered your purpose.

In the end, it takes time to discover your purpose; it won't happen in a few days, weeks, or months. You must do it one step at a time, which may take a lifetime.

It's also possible that your purpose evolves. Maybe you used to like working with animals, but now you'd prefer to support a cause that combats human trafficking. Alternatively, you may wish to pursue both, becoming one of the fortunate people whose lives are driven by more than one purpose.

Remember that finding your purpose does not always require you to stop doing what you currently do. Cutting hair could lead you to believe that making other people feel attractive is your calling in life. If you are a school custodian, you may discover that your job is to make the school atmosphere conducive to learning.

Now and again, think about stopping what you're doing to assess whether you're on the right track. You can alter your direction if not. Finding your calling sometimes involves navigating a few bends, forks, and stop signs.

Chapter 6: What Do I Want

One thing that most individuals want in life is to find a purpose. Whether we are aware of it or not. As appealing as it may sound, achieving it may not be easy.

You may have preconceived notions about the meaning of life if you haven't given it much thought to discover your purpose. These ingrained beliefs about life are frequently derived from our upbringing in our families and communities. Our life's work is to get married and start a family. Alternatively, it could be reaching a specific income target or standing in society.

However, the degree of fulfillment from discovering your sense of purpose is often lacking in these kinds of accomplishments. A personal sense of purpose has more of a continual effect on the world, massive or tiny, than a definite ultimate objective. Your reason is the purpose.

This feeling of self-purpose directs and maintains you, both on a daily and annual basis. Having a purpose in life provides stability and direction, even in the face of adversity and turbulence. For this reason, having a purpose in life is crucial to leading a happy and healthy existence. Even if it seems like a lofty question, it's essential to consider your goal and attempt to respond.

Discovering your purpose can achieve tremendous success and fulfillment in all facets of your life.

Now let's get down to business and discuss the key issues: what is your purpose, why is it important, and how do you discover your purpose in life?

What Is the Purpose of Life?

Philosophers have searched for and discussed "the purpose of life for thousands of years." Let's not attempt to address that here. Your life's purpose is what counts.

Many people will eventually wonder, "Why am I here?" The question can evoke fear or excitement. Leaning into the difficulty of this existential dilemma can lead to a more positive sense of self and more fulfilling paths forward.

Your life's mission is as distinct as your fingerprint. Everybody has unique gifts, life experiences, skill sets, and passions that make them shine. These are connected to your purpose, which is the reason you exist. You get out of bed in the morning despite the gloomy weather, your weariness, and your knowledge that the tasks and difficulties ahead will be complex or uninteresting.

This is not a short-term aim; the purpose is the long game. There's never an end to it. But having a strong sense of purpose isn't enough to keep you going. Because of this, your goal should ideally mesh with your passions and areas of interest.

This concept of "following your joy" is called *"ikigai"* in Japanese. In the West, *ikegai* has gained popularity recently as a means of assisting people in discovering their ideal vocations and career pathways.

Finding the intersection between your passion, what the world needs, and what you are good at—and what the world will pay for—is the idea behind this. You combine practical considerations with your passion to create your sense of purpose.

If fortune favors you, your career may have led you to discover your ikigai. For instance, a doctor should ideally feel their role is to aid the ill or lessen suffering.

Others find it more difficult to relate the meaning of their work to their sense of purpose. We often let go of the idealistic image of ourselves that longs to discover a sense of purpose and meaning in life due to work, family obligations, and social expectations. We think that to have meaning and purpose, we must make this trade-off with pragmatic reasons. It's not helpful, though.

You need a feeling of purpose to keep going over the long term. By pursuing what makes you happy and investing more time in it, you can still find and connect to your purpose, even when life seems like a series of compromises.

Why Is Finding Purpose Important?

Discovering your life's purpose may seem like a nice-to-have, but it's actually of greater importance than you might realize.

A meaningful life is associated with improved mental and physical well-being. Chronic disease risk is also decreased by it. It may even extend your life, according to numerous studies.

Being a part of a community is the foundation of having a purpose. While loneliness and solitude can lead to an existential crisis, using your abilities to serve others might help you discover your true meaning.

As you go through life, your purpose will likely shift. Maintaining your sense of purpose can be facilitated by ongoing development and advancement. Here's where self-discovery comes in.

What Does Self-Discovery Mean?

Understanding who you are—your values, your needs and desires, even your likes and dislikes in food—is the process of self-discovery. Some of these self-discovery insights may have come to you organically over time. However, many of us lose sight of our moral compass and keep our desires and impulses hidden—even from ourselves. Developing your self-discovery further can change your life.

Knowing your preferred meal or personality type is one thing. But the first step toward genuine self-discovery is to assess your life and consider what gives you energy and what doesn't. What will make your life happier? Why do you get out of bed in the mornings?

Once you've learned more about yourself, it will be simpler to identify your life's purpose and be who you indeed are in your personal and professional life. You will discover more about yourself if you realize what has been absent from your life.

However, don't expect to complete this trek in a single day. Self-discovery is a continuous endeavor. You must review every aspect of your life and give it some thought. To persevere through the process, you'll need bravery and resiliency since you might discover difficult aspects of yourself to embrace. [9]

It also takes a great deal of self-awareness, or self-knowledge, to discover your inner self. Generally speaking, self-knowledge relates to your awareness of your own emotions, convictions, and desires. Your ability to control your emotions will improve if you experience more of this. This will assist you in managing stress and enhancing your connections at work and in your personal life.

Gaining a deeper understanding of how the mind functions enhances empathy, creativity, self-control, and self-esteem. As a result, you'll even be more truthful.

Understanding how to begin a journey of self-discovery has countless advantages. Making the initial move and getting things going is what matters most.[10]

How To Start a Self-Discovery Journey?

The idea of setting out on a self-discovery adventure may scare you. How even do you start? The path to self-discovery is not predetermined. This implies that you can begin with any action that seems appropriate to you. Remember that starting this trip with courage is admirable, so maintain your momentum.

Although it may seem like an extensive, daunting idea, self-discovery is only just the process of:

---

[9] Shallcross L. (2010). A voyage of self-discovery.
https://ct.counseling.org/2010/01/a-voyage-of-self-discovery
[10] Schlegel RJ, et al. (2011). Feeling like you know who you are: Perceived true self-knowledge and meaning in life. DOI:
https://doi.org/10.1177/0146167211400424

- Contemplating your life.

- Determining what is absent.

- Moving in the direction of fulfillment.

The present is the ideal moment to begin self-exploration, so here are some pointers to get you going.

1. Start By Visualizing Your Ideal Self

Perhaps everything in your life has gone relatively well based on the advice that friends, parents, instructors, and other people have given you. If so, it's possible that you haven't given much attention to who you are.

Many people never consider the prospect of doing anything different; instead, they define themselves by their actions and interactions with others.

But if you don't know what matters to you or who you want to be, you'll keep living for other people rather than yourself.

As your trip is about figuring out the whole picture, you don't need to start with a finished picture. However, consider posing questions to yourself like these:

- What am I looking for in life?

- In five years, where do I see myself? Ten?

- What regrets do I have?

- What gives me pride in myself?

You can get started by looking at the answers to these queries. When you find yourself stuck, reflecting on what led up to a period in the past when you were content and joyful can be beneficial.

2. Explore Your Passions

Passions contribute to life's richness, significance, and sense of purpose.

Maybe your desire to serve others led you to pursue a medical career, but your work in medical billing doesn't fully satisfy that need.

Finding the job you truly desire and learning the procedures involved in making a career shift could be part of living out your passion. Or perhaps it's looking into volunteer opportunities using your street medical expertise.

Remember that passions don't always need to be technical or related to one's work. Consider your daily activities during your free time. What makes you happy and feels exciting?

Even pastimes like music and movies can provide perspective. You can find solutions to improve your life by reflecting on what you find enjoyable and look forward to doing most of the time.

3. Try New Things

Perhaps you have a limited list of passions. It's okay! You might not recall what you used to appreciate if you haven't cared for yourself in a while.

A helpful starting point for deciphering this? Try something novel and unique. You never know what you'll like until you try it, would you?

Perhaps you've always been interested in artistic endeavors, but after taking a pottery class in college, you never gave anything a go. Look for low-cost or free adult education programs at your neighborhood library or other community institutions.

Try using online lessons if you cannot attend a class in person. Even though they might not be identical, they can impart adequate knowledge to help you decide if you choose to keep up the pastime.

Trying out new interests, especially ones you haven't tried might occasionally seem overwhelming, mainly if you make the most daring choices.

If you're anxious, imagine how proud and successful you'll feel when you're done. Taking calculated risks[11] can increase your self-esteem and teach you more about yourself.

4. Evaluate Your Skills

Most people are naturally gifted in one or more areas, whether cooking, house repair, crafts, or any other talent. You may consider setting aside time to reflect on your unique skills and potential applications as part of your self-discovery journey.

Perhaps your neighbors frequently ask you for gardening advice, or your close friends always want you to organize their parties. Why not put these abilities into practice if you can see yourself mastering them?

---

[11] Felton A, et al. (2017). Therapeutic risk-taking: A justifiable choice. https://doi.org/10.1192/apt.bp.115.015701

By putting your abilities to use, you can improve them and boost your confidence. Consequently, increased self-assurance can motivate you to continue pursuing these skills and any others you might not have previously recognized.

5. Identify What You Value About Yourself

You can learn a lot about yourself by examining your values, which are the attributes you find most significant and essential. These principles can serve as an example of the kind of life you want to lead and the behavior you anticipate from others.

Values may include:

- honesty

- compassion

- loyalty

- creativity

- courage

- intelligence

By clarifying these values, you can ensure you are living up to them. Exploring your most valued beliefs in your self-discovery process can be pretty beneficial if you haven't done so before.

6. Ask Yourself Questions

To get answers, ask a few questions first.

- What motivates my actions?

- What drives me?

- What am I missing?

- What effect do my decisions have on the life I desire?

Next, use these inquiries in every aspect of your life.

However, don't feel pressured to have responses ready right away. Self-discovery is a process that takes time, so it's best to think through your answers thoroughly rather than just responding with the first thing that comes into your head.

Most importantly, be sincere with yourself. It's not a failure if you cannot find a suitable response. However, it does imply that some changes would be beneficial.

7. Learn Something New

Learning works best when it is viewed as an ongoing process.

Spend time studying the subject if it's something you've always wanted to know more about. You can learn much from books, manuals, and internet resources, particularly if you study scientific or historical concepts or build technical abilities.

Apps may help you start learning anything, from foreign languages to meditation, so search for it if you are interested. There's probably a free website or app for it.

Ultimately, increasing your knowledge is always a wise decision, regardless of whether you learn from a community member, enroll in a class, or teach yourself a new skill.

8. Keep A Journal

If you were a journal keeper in your teens, you may recall how it allowed you to examine your feelings and dreams. Resuming your journaling (or blogging) habit might assist you in reconnecting with yourself and discovering more about the person you've become.

A journal can be used for more valuable purposes besides self-reflection. You can delve deeper into any of the suggestions above or use your notebook to pose and answer questions.

You can monitor any recurring trends in your life by keeping a journal. Gaining additional knowledge about harmful patterns might be essential to self-discovery. You can start fixing it after you know what doesn't work.

You're not good at writing? That's acceptable. It can be helpful to write down anything that comes to mind.

A sketch diary or other art journal can also help explore your feelings and objectives if you have a stronger artistic inclination. Just put pen to paper, think about the future you want, and watch what emerges.

A psychotherapy approach called the "tombstone exercise"[12] might be something you want to give a try. It entails putting on paper your values and most significant accomplishments that you want to be remembered for when one looks down on your gravestone.

---

[12] Coleman S. (2015). Acceptance and commitment therapy: Tombstone exercise. http://www.thirdwavepsychotherapy.net/therapy/ewExternalFiles/tombstone%20exerc ise%20worksheet%2013-2-1.pdf

9. Talk To a Therapist

Therapy can offer a secure place to receive some compassionate direction when the journey of self-discovery feels overwhelming and you're not sure where to begin.[13]

It is not necessary to exhibit symptoms of mental illness to gain expert assistance. Counselors assist clients in resolving various problems, such as identity conflicts, career transitions, and goal clarification.

Although seeking self-awareness may not seem like a serious enough reason for counseling, therapy can be helpful if you're anxious or uneasy.

Five Benefits of Self-Discovery

For many people, the path to self-discovery will seem different. However, it has advantages that enable you to be who you are to everyone.

To help you put it into perspective, consider these five advantages that come with discovering who you are:

1. Your relationships will thrive

Your relationships will flourish with a clearer understanding of your fundamental beliefs and life goals. You'll be able to recognize harmful qualities in yourself or others and work

---

[13] LeJune JT, et al. (2016). Seven values "greatest hits": Our favorite values exercises from acceptance and commitment therapy.
https://portlandpsychotherapytraining.com/wp-content/uploads/sites/22/2016/06/Favorite_act_values_exercise_scripts.pdf

through more severe problems. Then, by being more forthright and honest, you can enhance your social well-being.

2. You'll experience less self-criticism

You'll understand that mistakes happen because we're human instead of berating ourselves for every error. It's not a reflection of your character. Also, you'll learn to steer clear of some blunders as you become more self-aware. Recognizing the reasons behind your mistakes is the first step towards avoiding them in the future.

3. You'll feel more creative

Being able to express yourself to others and develop your creativity depends on it. However, without knowing who you are, how can you express yourself? You can discover who you are and learn how to express it by engaging in self-reflection.[14]

4. You'll have a better ability to focus on what you truly want

Your journey of self-discovery is a continuous one that demands dedication and concentration. You'll be able to establish and accomplish goals with a stronger feeling of self-owing to that practice. You can create a future that truly represents you.

---

[14] Halloran L. (2016). The value of self-reflection. DOI: https://doi.org/10.1016/j.nurpra.2016.09.004

5. Your self-confidence will increase

Confidence in your skills and abilities can impact your personal and professional lives. Gaining self-assurance will enable you to approach new situations as a complete person rather than someone who fears difficulty or change. And when you go out on your path to better yourself, your confidence will only increase.

How To Keep Yourself Engaged with Your Self-Discovery Journey

You don't start and end self-discovery in a single afternoon. Reaching a point where you are satisfied with what you have learned may take several months, maybe a year or longer.

During that process, you can maintain your interest and learning in the following ways:

- Maintain organization in the pursuit of your personal and professional objectives.

- Look for diary prompts that will keep you thinking and stimulating.

- You can find inspiration by reading books, watching documentaries, and listening to podcasts about the experiences of others.

- Consider asking yourself, "Why am I drawn to these things?" or "What effect do I want my decisions to have on my life?"

Remember that discovering yourself and figuring out your life's purpose will be well worth the effort.

Bottomline is

Thinking about the future is not the only thing that comes with self-discovery. It also urges you to reflect on your history. Spending time thinking about prior emotions and events might be difficult. Never forget that asking your friends and relatives for assistance is acceptable.

Finding out where to start with self-discovery is just the first step. You'll have to step outside of your comfort zone and pose some challenging questions to yourself during this process. Take pride in yourself when you begin. You'll be happy you decided to connect with yourself more, and it's never too late.

Moreover, every successful individual has a clear sense of purpose. And you'll keep going through life as usual if you can't locate yours. You can get knocked off track and lost, not knowing which way to go or how to proceed. Alternately, even if everything in your life goes well, you can later look back and regret how you spent your time.

A well-rounded existence is built on discovering, accepting, and living out your purpose. It raises issues and concepts that some may find uncomfortable, but it takes some bravery. But it is worthwhile. Your sense of purpose gives you an internal compass to help you make decisions and point you toward the experiences that will enlighten your spirit.

Chapter 7: Be Relentless

We often sail through unknown oceans, encountering unforeseen storms that threaten to disrupt our goals in a world painted with the chaotic strokes of life's adversities. One constant light, nevertheless, shines through all of this uncertainty: the strength of our willpower and dedication to our goals.

Despite the difficulties, one cannot stress the importance of continuing this unwavering commitment. It is the cornerstone that dreams are built upon and the north star that keeps us company on the darkest nights. Even if they seem overwhelming, challenges put our commitment to the test and encourage us to have an unbreakable spirit.

This is not only a narrative but a wail for support and a reminder that we must remain steadfast in pursuing our ambitions regardless of how unpredictable life may get. The occurrence is a testament to never giving up and having trust in the human spirit's capacity. Our goals become inscribed deep into our hearts and souls through this unalterable want. Allow these words to strike a chord with you, kindling the flame of your aspirations, since it is through this steadfast desire that our dreams become engraved. What Impact Does Unforeseen Negative Circumstances Have On Our Life?

Unexpected events, seen as those sudden storms that worsen our lives' calmness, significantly impact our ambitions and overall well-being. These events are like the unforeseen guests that cause chaos when they arrive to meet us. These experiences—which may include anything from failures and unanticipated hardships to losses and setbacks—can drastically change our life trajectory.

Think about the suffering caused by an unexpected loss, maybe the death of a loved one. Our lives collapse momentarily, leaving huge voids where love and support previously stood. The emotional storm after losing someone is uncontrollably intense, disrupting our hearts' peace and creating a hole that is hard to fill.

Moreover, we can see these unforeseen circumstances as deviations from our planned goals in life or setbacks, which have an influence that is distinct but no less powerful. They put our capacity to navigate through unfamiliar terrain to the test, challenging the fundamental foundation of our resilience. Unforeseen circumstances like a successful business going bankrupt or an unanticipated medical disease can move our lives to the core.

These events have a significant emotional cost as well. It blurs out life's goals and ambitions with the shadow of hopelessness. It sets off a range of emotional responses, such as anger, frustration, sadness, or a jumble of contradictory feelings in our heads. Mentally, these shockwaves might confuse us, making us doubt our previously well-laid plans and wonder whether we are here.

To understand it better, imagine you have failed in your career or have faced a substantial financial loss. These types of unforeseen incidents create challenges that hurt us the most. Our human mind can barely handle any career failure with grace. Since we have been working for a specific job for years now, we have put our dedication and hard work into it, but now it is not working for us anymore, so we have to reassess our passion and adjust our careers accordingly. Similarly, enduring financial loss would abandon our future dreams, forcing us to shift our priorities. You might have planned to buy a home for yourself after years of hard work, but you incurred a loss in your business deal recently. It all happens for a reason; we have to be patient.

These unforeseen occurrences reroute our paths; sometimes, we must redirect our goals that demand resilience and strength of mind. These events make us formulate our timelines repeatedly; they redraw our blueprints and push the essence of our determination.

No matter how disruptive these unforeseen unfavorable circumstances are, we cannot let them define us. Instead, we should take these circumstances as an open invitation to showcase the extent of our resilience, patience, and our hidden spirit. While they overshadow our ongoing path, they also give us opportunities for courage, growth, and the endless pursuit of our aims while facing adversity.

The Power of Resilience

Being an unbeatable force within our spirits, resilience serves as a ray of hope in the middle of storms of life. It embodies the unhesitating resolution to thrive, adapt, and keep up with our goals in the face of misfortune, beating the unbreakable chains of circumstance.[15] At its core, resilience is our protector against the offensive episodes of life, an inner resistance that helps us when the world appears to collapse. Its importance lies not only in calming the storms of our life but in coming out from it, modified and courageous.

Countless narratives exist to have an idea of testaments to the powerfulness of resilience.[16] Consider Helen Keller's story, who challenged her weakness of deafness and blindness, showing the world with her unbeatable spirit. Her tale showcases strength— rising above physical boundaries to attain the art of intellectual and emotional stability.

Similarly, the inspiring story of Nelson Mandela creates a considerable impression of resilience in the face of elongated hardships. Despite years of imprisonment, his spirits remain high, and he came out from jail intact, reflecting forgiveness and stability in his behavior in pursuit of equality and justice.

These experiences of people remind us that resilience is more than a mere abstract theory. It is a substantial power that pushes people beyond their limits, especially when faced with unforeseen and adverse circumstances. It surpasses hurdles, motivating people to reroute their paths, rewrite their stories, and change sharp stones into stepping blocks to move forward.

---

[15] Wu, Yin, Zhi-qin Sang, Xiao-Chi Zhang, and Jürgen Margraf. "The relationship between resilience and mental health in Chinese college students: a longitudinal cross-lagged analysis." Frontiers in psychology 11 (2020): 108.
[16] Feldman, Ruth. "What is resilience: an affiliative neuroscience approach." World psychiatry 19, no. 2 (2020): 132-150.

From a psychological perspective, resilience serves as a lifeboat among the most formidable waves of the ocean. It instills a feeling of optimism and flexibility while strengthening the mind against hopelessness. It uses the power of thinking to help us see obstacles as chances for personal development rather than insurmountable obstacles. Resilience, however, provides a way through suffering; it does not eliminate it. Resilient people can push beyond the hurt that bad things have done to them and keep moving forward. It's not about brushing off feelings; instead, it's about mastering them and accepting grief without letting them control how we live.

There are several ways to foster resilience, which can provide light throughout life's darkest moments. Building a network of friends, mentors, or the community around you may be a lifeline in trying times. It gives perspectives different from our own, fostering a feeling of community and offering consolation and direction. Furthermore, cultivating flexibility is essential to resilience. Accepting change and using adaptable strategies in the face of difficulty strengthens our capacity to pass through the tough times of life.

Resilience is developed via mindfulness exercises like meditation and introspection, which promote emotional control and clarity in the face of turmoil. They operate as teachers, bringing us back on track and enabling us to respond to difficulties to solve them rather than react to them.

Moreover, resilient people are motivated by maintaining a sense of purpose. A strong vision and objectives give life purpose and serve as a beacon of hope even in the darkest of circumstances. Being resilient means overcoming adversity stronger, more innovative, and more caring than just getting through a storm. It's the skill of turning hardship into a chance for development, a monument to the boundless persistence of the human spirit. It calls us to rise to life's most significant difficulties and adapt and prosper in the face of them.

Why Should We Adapt to Change when facing unforeseen circumstances?

Change is one thing that is consistent in life, which often surprises us and transforms our daily routine. Accepting the value of flexibility while facing unforeseen events serves as a light to help us navigate life's difficult moments. Our capacity to change our behavior, adjust to the current situation, and adapt is a sign of resilience and bravery.

It becomes crucial to modify plans when we experience a few unexpected difficulties without losing sight of long-term objectives. This requires striking a careful balance between being adaptable to the path chosen and being dedicated to the final goal. The methods required for this adjustment need a combination of vision and pragmatism.[17]

First, it becomes crucial to reframe our perceptions. Consider changes as diversions that provide different ways to achieve the same objective rather than as obstacles to be overcome. This change in perspective enables us towards a more flexible strategy, allowing us to take on new challenges without losing sight of our main goals. Furthermore, using a proactive approach works wonders. Being able to anticipate possible changes and

---

[17] Mithani, Murad A. "Adaptation in the face of the new normal." Academy of Management Perspectives 34, no. 4 (2020): 508-530.

have backup plans helps us deal with uncertainty. Planning with flexibility makes sure that obstacles are seen as chances for creativity rather than unbearable difficulties.

Embracing change becomes a transformative experience when we see it as a catalyst for our personal growth. It entices us to step out of our comfort zones and foster resilience and adaptability. Every unexpected turn becomes a life-long lesson, enriching our journey toward our future aspirations.

How To Take Over Control While Facing Adversity?

People have an innate power when faced with chaotic circumstances in life. That power shows their ability to choose how to respond to particular circumstances.[18] Managing this reaction is essential to directing our energy through hardships. However, mastering our responses to outside events is more important than trying to control them.

Despite being seen as a barrier, adversity has the unexplored capacity to encourage advancement. It serves as a catalyst, fueling our resolve and enabling us to move forward with our plans and objectives. Resilient people use this misfortune as inspiration rather than giving in to hopelessness.[19]

---

[18] Scheffers, Femke, Eveline van Vugt, and Xavier Moonen. "Resilience in the face of adversity in adults with an intellectual disability: A literature review." Journal of Applied Research in Intellectual Disabilities 33, no. 5 (2020): 828-838.
[19] Shepherd, Dean A., Fouad Philippe Saade, and Joakim Wincent. "How to circumvent adversity? Refugee-entrepreneurs' resilience in the face of substantial and persistent adversity." Journal of Business Venturing 35, no. 4 (2020): 105940.

Adversity's transforming power comes from its capacity to provoke reflection.[20] It makes us rethink our approaches, convictions, and assets. It ignites a fire within us, requiring a greater will to overcome challenges and a more profound devotion to objectives. Adversity also fosters creativity and ingenuity. It forces us to think creatively and unconventionally, encouraging inventiveness and resourcefulness. Adversity's obstacles are stepping stones that lead us to potential areas where development is abundant.

Essentially, the reaction that is fostered post-hardship is what holds the power, not the difficulty itself. It calls on us to rise above our circumstances and use them as fuel for resiliency, development, and, ultimately, achieving our goals. When adversity is used as fuel, failures become foundations for unlimited accomplishments.

Adopting a Relentless Mindset

Within the complexities of our existence lies the ability to foster a relentless mindset. This unbeatable force guides us toward our goals despite the difficulties in life that are stopping us. This mindset isn't just a characteristic but a responsive development, a dedication to carry on with life against all odds.[21]

An unstoppable, relentless mindset enables us to face obstacles with our heads high and overcome them with courage

---

[20] Read, John, and David J. Harper. "The power threat meaning framework: Addressing adversity, challenging prejudice and stigma, and transforming services." Journal of Constructivist Psychology 35, no. 1 (2022): 54-67.
[21] Clancy, Annette. "The Growth Mindset." Accountancy Ireland (2020).

and resiliency.[22] Perseverance is fueled by an unyielding drive to overcome difficult situations in life. This mentality reinterprets failures as brief diversionary routes instead of unresolved obstacles. It imparts the idea that failure is a necessary step on the path to achievement rather than the final destination. Adopting this perspective makes people feel invincible and empowers them to face challenges any time life throws at them.

Tips and Techniques for Cultivating a Relentless Mindset

1. Clarity of Purpose

Clearly define your objectives. Every choice and action is guided by this clarity, which serves as a North Star.

2. Resilience Through Challenges

Reframe obstacles as chances for development. Accept failures as teaching opportunities and sources of creativity.

3. Adopting a Growth Mindset

Accept the concept that intelligence and skill can be acquired. Also, failures should be seen as opportunities rather than obstacles.

4. Positive Self-Talk

Have a constructive internal discussion with your inner self. Boost your self-esteem and affirmation while facing challenges.

---

[22] Avil Beckford, "What Does It Mean to Be Relentless, Are You Relentless?," The Invisible Mentor, March 27, 2022, https://theinvisiblementor.com/what-does-it-mean-to-be-relentless-are-you-relentless/.

Practical Exercises to Strengthen Determination

1. Visualization

Visualize yourself succeeding. Visualization methods strengthen resolve by giving the impression that accomplishment is realistic and possible.

2. Daily Affirmations

Write empowering phrases that support your objectives. A resilient attitude is strengthened by regular repetition of these affirmations.[23]

3. Challenging Comfort Zones

Don't hesitate to leave your comfort zone. Accepting pain promotes adaptation and resilience.

4. Mindfulness Practices

Engage in mindfulness activities like meditation or journaling. These practices enhance self-awareness and emotional regulation, strengthening resilience.24

Relentlessness is more than simply a way of thinking; it's a tool that helps people reach their goals and unlock milestones.[25]

---

[23] Albalooshi, Sumaya, Mehrad Moeini-Jazani, Bob M. Fennis, and Luk Warlop. "Reinstating the resourceful self: when and how self-affirmations improve executive performance of the powerless." Personality and Social Psychology Bulletin 46, no. 2 (2020): 189-203.

[24] Griffiths, Austin, David Royse, April Murphy, and Saundra Starks. "Self-care practice in social work education: A systematic review of interventions." Journal of Social Work Education 55, no. 1 (2019): 102-114.

[25] Avil Beckford, "What Does It Mean to Be Relentless, Are You Relentless?," The Invisible Mentor, March 27, 2022, https://theinvisiblementor.com/what-does-it-mean-to-be-relentless-are-you-relentless/.

It is the power that guarantees every failure is a teaching moment and every obstacle a chance for improvement. People with a persistent attitude get momentum by persevering through difficulties and being dedicated to the path. They change course, adapt, innovate, and use obstacles as catalysts to advance.

This thinking cultivates an enduring perseverance that makes every action, no matter how little, add to achievement in the grand scheme of things. The difference between those who only dream and those who succeed is persistence. In the end, having a persistent attitude is a manner of life rather than just a strategy for reaching objectives. It molds mindsets, behaviors, and processes, giving every undertaking an unwavering spirit. Adopting this mentality is essential to reaching tremendous heights and discovering the unrealized potential of others.

How Important Is It To Stay Committed To The Plan?

Amidst life's turbulent twists and turns, the ethos of victory lies not just in making a plan to protect ourselves from more considerable loss when faced with something unusual but purposeful, staying devoted to it, firmly sailing through the storms of life that threaten to destroy our path.[26]

Sticking to the plan while facing difficulties is a sign of resilience as much as willpower. It's the realization that obstacles, no matter how big or strong, are just temporary stones in our life-long journey to accomplish our dreams. With this

---

[26] Framework, Planning, Housing Needs, Saanich Housing Needs, Housing Strategy, Saanich Housing Strategy, and Vision Quarter. "Update the "How to Use this Plan" for consistency across all LAPs, Corridor and Action Plans." Policy 6, no. 3: 85.

mindset, every obstacle becomes a chance for development, grit, and unshakable dedication.

It's in our best interest to recall the overarching goal and the long-term picture, which serves as a beacon of hope that helps us navigate tough life. It serves as a light throughout the darkest times, reminding us of the importance of our goals beyond temporary failures. This long-term vision encompasses more than individual goals; it goes beyond personal achievement to include our impact on others. It's about making a lasting impression, motivating others, clearing the path for an infinitely bright future for ourselves, and becoming a role model for our younger generation.[27]

Rewards and Personal Growth Achieved by Relentlessness

The benefits of tireless dedication go beyond just achieving set objectives of life.[28] They capture the essence of our journey itself, including the changes, developments, and opportunities for personal growth that arise. Not only that, but the rewards also reach the level of personal contentment. Knowing that each challenge faced and every setback conquered is evidence of one's everlasting devotion brings great pleasure. The satisfaction comes from understanding that giving up is never an option.

Being persistent means developing into someone capable of reaching those milestones, not merely one who chases after them. The character is made in the furnace of adversity—the

---

[27] Framework, Planning, Housing Needs, Saanich Housing Needs, Housing Strategy, Saanich Housing Strategy, and Vision Quarter. "Update the "How to Use this Plan" for consistency across all LAPs, Corridor and Action Plans." Policy 6, no. 3: 85.
[28] Leary, Mark R., and Shira Gabriel. "The relentless pursuit of acceptance and belonging." In Advances in motivation science, vol. 9, pp. 135-178. Elsevier, 2022.

resiliency, grit, and resolve that seep into one's essence. Continuous dedication shows results through achievement and leaves a lasting impression on the chosen path. It encourages a culture of resiliency and endurance by motivating others to aspire to the unshakable resolve shown. Moreover, the influence transcends individual confines and affects domains outside one's area. It becomes a force for transformation, demonstrating the transforming potential of unwavering persistence.

In short, agreement to the plan itself is a significant part of your journey instead of just attaining a set of goals. It shows the existence of perseverance, strength, and determined courage while facing the most challenging times in life. It exemplifies the cliché that being successful is an adventure instead of a destination, and it is at the core of the concept. It is the procedure of existing, evolving, and emerging beyond the limitations imposed on oneself by the circumstances. The unwavering dedication changes our lives and leaves a legacy—making ambitions more than hopes and dreams.

It would help to embrace loneliness as a gift rather than a burden. An opportunity to change the course of your life. It works as the canvas where dreams come true, failures are stepping stones for success, and hardships spur perseverance.[29]

Allow determination to penetrate your goals, give your every action a sense of purpose, and drive you forward as you get closer to your desires. In this unrelenting hunt, the ordinary becomes exceptional when dreams come true and ambitions

---

[29] Leary, Mark R., and Shira Gabriel. "The relentless pursuit of acceptance and belonging." In Advances in motivation science, vol. 9, pp. 135-178. Elsevier, 2022.

become distant visions.[30] Let perseverance guide you as you progress towards your next milestone. Let it be the voice that gives you suggestions when you're feeling doubtful, the compass that helps you find your way through the uncertainty, and the unshakable force that pushes you to the top of achievement.

Accept it, tend to it, and allow it to become woven into your identity. Because there is an unparalleled ability to change not just your life but also the lives of others who see the unwavering force of endurance when you embrace relentlessness, may your steadfast determination serve as your beacon of light, your constant companion on the road to greatness, and the impetus that pushes you to rise above the ordinary and embrace the exceptional.

It would be best if you embraced relentlessness not as a burden but as a gift—an invitation to rewrite the narratives of your lives. It's the canvas upon which aspirations transform into achievements, where setbacks are springboards for growth, and adversities become catalysts for resilience.

Let relentlessness permeate your aspirations, infuse every step with determination, and propel you forward, steadfastly inching closer to your dreams. In this relentless pursuit, the ordinary transcends into the extraordinary, where aspirations cease to be distant mirages and materialize as tangible realities.[31] As you embark on the journey ahead, let relentlessness be your

---

[30] Tony Fahkry, "Why It Pays to Be Relentless in the Game of Life," Medium, January 4, 2018, https://medium.com/the-mission/why-it-pays-to-be-relentless-in-the-game-of-life-414c4f59d46e.

[31] Tony Fahkry, "Why It Pays to Be Relentless in the Game of Life," Medium, January 4, 2018, https://medium.com/the-mission/why-it-pays-to-be-relentless-in-the-game-of-life-414c4f59d46e.

ally. Let it be the voice that whispers encouragement when doubts surface, the compass guiding you through the maze of uncertainties, and the unwavering force propelling you toward the peak of success.

Embrace, nurture, and let it weave into the very part of your being. In the embrace of relentlessness lies the unrivaled potential to transform not just your life but the lives of those who witness the sheer power of perseverance. May relentlessness be your guiding light, your unwavering companion on the path to greatness, and the force that propels you to transcend the ordinary and embrace the extraordinary.

Chapter 8: Ask For Help

Knowing, your ambition is like driving a car to reach your destination, but the roads are unfamiliar. It's the motivation, the enthusiasm, the intense desire to do something meaningful.[32] This is a sentiment that many young people can relate to; they have goals and ideas that shine brightly in their thoughts, yet the route to making these wishes come true often appears blurry.

Being ambitious without a plan might be likened to being lost in a thick forest with similar routes everywhere. The goal is there, and the destination is known, but the means of getting there still need to be determined.[33] It's a frequent problem that often leaves people feeling helpless and overwhelmed.

The first step is to have a clear vision in life, and the next step needs clarity. Clarity marks the path to the desired destination. It's about knowing "what" to do but asking for help with "how." Many people struggle at this point because they are afraid to voice their doubts or ask for assistance navigating the new territory of their dreams. Clarity is the compass that directs your

---

[32] Stanciu, Theodora. "How to Ask for Help at Work." How to Ask for Help at Work, November 16, 2023. https://mirro.io/blog/the-leaders-approach/.
[33] "Setting and Identifying Goals." Campus Health, May 23, 2022. https://campushealth.unc.edu/health-topic/setting-and-identifying-goals/.

ambitious ship in the proper direction. It's about grasping the details and dissecting the magnificent vision into more manageable benchmarks. However, it also involves recognizing the limits of one's knowledge and experience and admitting that, even if your ambitions may seem obvious, getting there may be easier with the guidance and expertise of others.

The value of clarity while creating goals must be emphasized more. It is the foundation upon which the success is built. But it's also critical to recognize that asking for assistance is a sign of strength, not weakness, and that it shows how committed one is to realize their dreams.

For several young people, the easiest thing is putting their goals into words. They see themselves in prosperous occupations, fulfilling relationships, stable finances, or personal development.[34] However, the path to realizing these goals is often still being determined when asking for advice and support from others becomes quite essential.

Many people around the globe have walked similar roads to our own. Asking for their advice is beneficial. It's not only about learning new things; it's also about taking lessons from their failures, successes, and priceless life lessons.

Clarity arises in life goal setting not just from inside but also from other people's opinions and experiences. It's about accepting common knowledge that can show the way forward. Understanding ambition and finding clarity are the foundations

---

[34] Schippers, Michaéla C., and Niklas Ziegler. "Life crafting as a way to find purpose and meaning in life." Frontiers in Psychology 10 (2019): 2778.

that keep one going while pursuing objectives.[35] They signal the importance of understanding that, while desire feeds the dream, asking for advice and assistance shows how to transform such aspirations into concrete, attainable realities.

The Power of Vulnerability

Have you ever wondered why it gets difficult for us to seek help? Why do we link asking for support with weakness and vulnerability? In my journey of self-discovery and achievement, I've learned that the most remarkable battles often occur within, especially when shattering the stereotype that seeking help signifies weakness. This stereotype, deeply ingrained in our societal psyche, is like a formidable wall that many, including myself, struggle to overcome.[36] However, the truth I've discovered is quite the opposite – asking for help is an act of courage and strength.

Almost every individual acts in a certain way when they need emotional help; they will be willing to provide it instead of taking it when needed.[37] Because of our society's stigma of perfectionism, we ask each other, "How are you?" with the intention of hearing, "I am great, thanks!".

---

[35] Stanciu, Theodora. "How to Ask for Help at Work." How to Ask for Help at Work, November 16, 2023. https://mirro.io/blog/the-leaders-approach/.
[36] Tsai, Mavis, David Yoo, Emerson J. Hardebeck, Mary Plummer Loudon, and Robert J. Kohlenberg. "Creating safe, evocative, attuned, and mutually vulnerable therapeutic beginnings: Strategies from functional analytic psychotherapy." Psychotherapy 56, no. 1 (2019): 55.
[37] Garcia, Corinne. "The Courage of Vulnerability: Asking for Help." Heartmanity Blog, 2023. https://blog.heartmanity.com/the-courage-of-vulnerability-asking-for-help#:~:text=As%20Bren%C3%A9%20Brown%20in%20%22The,a%20willingness%20to%20be%20transparent.

We all have faked this question because if we tell people how we feel at that moment, we can appear sad or confused; we give the ideal answer to save ourselves from expressing our emotional side.[38] However, sharing our genuine emotions will only show our strong emotional intelligence and help us be transparent.

Recognizing the Right People to Ask for Help

Finding the appropriate resources for support is just as important as asking for it when pursuing personal and professional development.[39] It can create a difference between taking a step forward to attain your goal and missing an opportunity to know the right person to approach. There are many helpers out there, each providing unique insights and resources. Comprehending these types and assessing the assistance that best fits your requirements will be valuable for your success.

Professionals: They are specialists in specific fields. Consider financial advisers, career coaches, legal consultants, and therapists. Their counseling is grounded on a thorough knowledge of their industry. You must consult professionals regarding specific information, such as financial planning, mental health issues, or legal difficulties.

Mentors: These people have already walked the same journey as you. They provide insight gleaned from experience,

---

[38] Stanciu, Theodora. "How to Ask for Help at Work." How to Ask for Help at Work, November 16, 2023. https://mirro.io/blog/the-leaders-approach/.

[39] Grant, Heidi. "The Right Way to Ask for Help at Work." Harvard Business Review, July 8, 2018. https://hbr.org/2018/05/how-to-get-the-help-you-need.

direction, encouragement, and often a much-needed reality check. Someone with extensive expertise in the areas you want to succeed in, such as a professor or a senior professional in your industry, may serve as a mentor. They are perfect for providing long-term direction, assisting with career path navigation, or assisting with life-altering choices.

Family Members: Our family provides practical advice, emotional support, and a distinct perspective, sometimes based on their experiences. They do not give professional advice, but they provide you with advice with personal care and compassion because they have a deep love for us.

Peers: These people are at the same stage of life or work as you. They show compassion and kindness, often lending a sympathetic shoulder or a listening ear.[40] Peer support is essential for emotional support, experience sharing, and learning from each other's mistakes and accomplishments.

The appropriate resource of support may change based on your circumstances. A professional or mentor may be a better choice for matters about your career. You could get the help you need from a family member or peer if you're having emotional difficulties or issues in your personal life. The secret is to evaluate your circumstances, determine the kind of assistance you need, and then ask for help from the right person.[41] By doing this, you create a broad, experienced, and empathetic support network in addition to gaining insightful knowledge.

---

[40] Stanciu, Theodora. "How to Ask for Help at Work." How to Ask for Help at Work, November 16, 2023. https://mirro.io/blog/the-leaders-approach/.

[41] Grant, Heidi. "The Right Way to Ask for Help at Work." Harvard Business Review, July 8, 2018. https://hbr.org/2018/05/how-to-get-the-help-you-need.

How to Ask For Guidance?

You must craft the questions to achieve success and grow personally. It refers to conversing about what you want and clearly, which is also receptive and open to the support you can receive. This skill ensures that the help you seek is effective, relevant, and transformative.[42]

The first step in effectively seeking guidance is to communicate your needs. This involves introspection and clarity about what you are asking for.

1. Be Specific: General requests like "I need help with my career" are too vague. Be specific about your needs. For instance, "I need advice on transitioning to a career in graphic design" is a clearer ask.

2. State Your Goals: Explain what you hope to achieve with the help you seek. Knowing your end goal allows the helper to offer more targeted and valuable advice.

3. Contextualize Your Request: Provide background information to help the person understand your situation. This context makes your request more relatable and easier to address.

4. Ask Questions: Come up with specific questions. This shows that you've thought about your situation and makes it easier for the person to provide concrete advice.

---

[42] Stanciu, Theodora. "How to Ask for Help at Work." How to Ask for Help at Work, November 16, 2023. https://mirro.io/blog/the-leaders-approach/.

5. Be Vocal About Your Circumstances: Don't downplay or exaggerate your circumstances. Honesty ensures that the advice you receive is appropriate and valuable.[43]

It's critical to be open and responsive to the advice and direction you get once you've expressed your concerns. Now, you need to accept viewpoints that may diverge from your own. Diverse perspectives can provide fresh ideas and solutions. You also have to listen carefully to what is being stated. To listen actively, one must hear what is being said and comprehend the meaning and emotions underlying it.

Feel free to ask for clarity if anything needs to be clarified. Asking for an explanation demonstrates your interest and desire to learn. However, you must recognize that the individual is giving you their time to assist you. Whether their advice is what you were hoping for or it is not helpful, show gratitude for their help. Take some time to consider the advice you've been given. Examine how well it suits your needs and how you may use it.

Asking for support is about starting a meaningful conversation, not simply knowing what to do. Clear communication and an open, responsive mentality go hand in hand and provide the foundation for insightful mentoring and successful relationships. Gaining proficiency in these skills exposes you to a plethora of information and experience that may help you achieve your final objectives.

---

[43] Stanciu, Theodora. "How to Ask for Help at Work." How to Ask for Help at Work, November 16, 2023. https://mirro.io/blog/the-leaders-approach/.

Showing Gratitude In Your Actions

The art of gratitude, especially when acknowledging the help received, is essential to positive relationships and personal growth. This skill is not just a social subtlety but an intense depiction that boosts mutual respect, deepens connections, and builds an environment of positive exchange. You can show gratitude in many ways.

1. Personalized Appreciation: A simple 'thank you' often falls flat. Make your gratitude personalized to make it more meaningful. Mention specific aspects of how their advice or assistance was beneficial to you.

2. Timeliness: Express your thanks soon after receiving help. Timely gratitude shows that you are attentive and genuinely appreciate the assistance rendered.

3. Public Acknowledgement: It is essential to appreciate the advisor in public whenever you get a chance because it will make them feel good about themselves, and they might continue sharing their advice with others, too. It can also be beneficial for their image or professional development.

4. Sincerity: Be sincere in your thanks. People can easily discern between perfunctory thanks and genuine appreciation.

5. Small Gestures: You can send a heartfelt message, a simple note, or any little gift or flowers as your expression of admiration towards them.

Helping Others In A Similar Manner

Although gratitude is essential, going above and offering reciprocal assistance turns appreciation into a positive feedback loop that fosters community development. After receiving aid, you must seek chances to help others. This does not imply that you have to contribute similarly; instead, help where you are competent and comfortable. You may also impart the knowledge and resources you've acquired by receiving assistance helping not just other people but also confirms your comprehension and gratitude for the assistance you were given.

If you are in a position where you can be a mentor to someone who is looking out for help, be one. Remember when you wanted a mentor and how it made you feel when you got the help you sought? It is one of the best ways to reciprocate support and wisdom to society. Similarly, creating an atmosphere where asking for and providing assistance is recognized and encouraged is crucial, whether in business or social settings.

Positivity in relationships is reflected when you are grateful for the assistance received and offer reciprocal help to others. It creates networks, strengthens ties, and creates a supportive environment where individuals may flourish. By developing the skill of gratitude, you may foster a culture of support for one another and ongoing development, in addition to demonstrating your feelings for the assistance you have received.

Transformation of Your Path After Seeking Help

Your life can experience a transformation when you ask for help. It enables you to seek immediate support and provide long-term advantages, initiating personal growth and benefitting future decision-making.[44]

Seeking assistance has long-term advantages that go beyond solving an issue right away. It encourages an open-minded and ongoing learning mindset. People who adopt this strategy are more robust, adaptive, and ready to take on new challenges. They discover the significance of many viewpoints and that knowledge may originate from various sources.

Furthermore, the connections from offering support are usually based on mutual respect and are a strong pillar in your growth. These relationships are a building block of your journey, offering advice, opportunities, and otherwise inaccessible resources. Most of the time, these connections become our lifetime mentors and turn into our sincere friends.

The act of seeking help also enhances decision-making skills. Exposure to different viewpoints and advice provides a broader base of knowledge and experience to draw from when making future decisions. It encourages thorough consideration and consultation, leading to more informed and effective choices.

Embracing New Relationships and Creating a Support Network

Establishing and maintaining a support system via networking is crucial for pursuing professional and personal success. Building sincere connections that offer opportunity, support, and direction is more critical than just growing your network of

---

[44] Schippers, Michaéla C., and Niklas Ziegler. "Life crafting as a way to find purpose and meaning in life." Frontiers in Psychology 10 (2019): 2778.

contacts. When this community is sustained and developed over time, it forms a basis for ongoing success and progress.

Building Connections for Personal Growth

When seeking assistance, you make new connections without knowing it. Every assistance attempt is a chance to contact someone who can be very important to our personal development. [45]For example, contacting a mentor may help you grow your network by introducing you to them while offering rapid guidance. Similarly, you can meet people with similar issues and ambitions by joining a professional group or community.

These relationships are more than contact list names; they are practical friends, mentors, and companions. For instance, a workshop participant and you may collaborate on a project after initiating a casual conversation. Alternatively, a mentoring connection may develop into a sustained business collaboration.

This kind of networking is about creating a supportive community where people can learn from and support one another's experiences, abilities, and ideas.[46] This community becomes a source of fresh viewpoints, ideas, and possibilities, enabling development that would not have been achievable.

Nevertheless, keeping these connections lasting beyond the first conversation is essential. Here are a few suggestions for maintaining and fostering these relationships:

---

[45] James, Ranu. "Weaving stories of culture and connection." Educating Young Children 27, no. 2 (2021): 12-15.

[46] Hengelbrok, Helena, and Edward L. Baker. "Connecting with coaches, mentors, and sponsors: advice for the emerging leader." Journal of Public Health Management and Practice 27, no. 4 (2021): 421-423.

1. Regular Communication: By staying in touch almost daily, even if it's just a brief hi-hello or sharing a blog that interests you. This helps keep the relationship active and shows that you value the connection.

2. Genuine Interest: Show genuine interest in their achievements and projects. Join them in their successes and be there for them during tough times.

3. Reciprocity: You need to find ways to give it back. If someone has helped you, think about how you can assist them. It doesn't need to be the same effort; it could be just offering feedback for their actions, supporting their work, or lending them a listening ear when needed.

4. Networking Events: Attend networking events and invite your contacts, helping maintain your relationship and providing them with networking opportunities.

5. Personal Touch: Remember personal details and occasions like birthdays or anniversaries. A personal touch goes a long way in strengthening relationships.

6. Consistency: You should stay consistent while making efforts for the other person. These connections take time to develop and demand continuous care.

The process of creating and maintaining a support system is dynamic. It's all about establishing and maintaining connections that benefit both parties. These relationships, built by asking for assistance, grow to be a great asset and serve as a basis for success, understanding, and ongoing development. This network grows as you advance in both your personal and professional life, serving as a monument to the strength of community and cooperation in accomplishing objectives.

82

Chapter 9: Your Consistent Actions

A commitment, in simple words, is an enforceable promise or vow made to oneself or another.[47] The ability to remain steadfast while facing adversity is what we mean when we refer to commitment. It's about not deviating while facing difficulties and sticking to our goals and choices without mistakes. If we talk about personal development, then making a promise to ourselves that we must work hard towards achieving growth is what we call commitment.[48]

Conversely, behavioral consistency refers to consistently matching our actions with our ideas and commitments over time.[49] It pertains to consistently following a particular path to achieve our objectives while exhibiting consistent actions that align with our core beliefs and ambitions. Consistency is the underlying element. That connects our endeavors, forming a cohesive narrative of advancement and success.

---

[47] Turner, Christopher O. Stress Over the Life Course: A Qualitative Analysis of Graduate Students' Stress and Commitment During the Graduate Career. Indiana University, 2020.
[48] Knowles, Susanne, and Susanne Knowles. "Coaching for Self-Awareness and Insight." Positive Psychology Coaching (2021): 117-126.
[49] Feng, Tiantian, and Shrikanth S. Narayanan. "Modeling behavioral consistency in large-scale wearable recordings of human bio-behavioral signals." In ICASSP 2020-2020 IEEE International Conference on Acoustics, Speech and Signal Processing (ICASSP), pp. 1011-1015. IEEE, 2020.

For young adults, these concepts are incredibly fundamental to personal development. This period of life is often marked by exploration, identity formation, and laying foundations for the future. Here, commitment is an anchor, providing a sense of direction amid the tumult of possibilities and choices. It enables young adults to navigate the complex waters of burgeoning independence, societal pressures, and various paths available.

Behavioral consistency acts as a guiding principle at this formative time. Young adults are now in the phase of defining their identity and principles.[50] Consistent actions strengthen self-perception and establish a dependable framework of habits and behaviors that uphold their long-term objectives. The maintenance of this consistency is vital in a world that is more characterized by rapidity and volatility. It implies that while having internal and internal uncertainties, a consistent pattern of acts and choices aligns with one's fundamental principles.

Furthermore, commitment and consistency are closely connected to developing resilience and self-efficacy. Adhering to their obligations instructs young people to overcome challenges and recover from failures. They discover that achieving achievement and experiencing progress often result from persistence and the gradual accumulation of regular, diligent endeavors rather than occasional bursts of intensity.

---

[50] Wickham, Shay-Ruby, Natasha A. Amarasekara, Adam Bartonicek, and Tamlin S. Conner. "The big three health behaviors and mental health and well-being among young adults: a cross-sectional investigation of sleep, exercise, and diet." Frontiers in Psychology 11 (2020): 579205.

Role of Self-Perception in Shaping Our Lives

Self-perception is a strong, often unintentional force that directs our activities and molds our behavior.[51] It refers to our perception, which encompasses our talents, perspective, and inherent worth in addition to our outward appearance. This force dramatically impacts our opinions about the world and alters how we react to challenging times.

The concept of self-perception is intrinsically linked to the self-fulfilling prophecy phenomenon. This is where our beliefs about ourselves influence our actions to such an extent that we essentially bring these beliefs to life. For instance, if a young adult believes they are inherently bad at public speaking, they may avoid opportunities to speak, or when they do speak, they might be so anxious and unprepared that they perform poorly, reinforcing their initial belief.[52] This cycle can trap individuals in a pattern that perpetually confirms their negative self-perceptions.

Comprehending the significant correlation between thinking and acting is essential, particularly for young people shaping their social trajectories. Possessing a good self-perception may help us move forward and achieve happiness while having a poor self-perception might hinder us from achieving anything.[53] We must

---

[51] Morina, N., 2021. Comparisons inform me who I am: A general comparative-processing model of self-perception. Perspectives on Psychological Science, 16(6), pp.1281-1299.

[52] Palenzuela-Luis, Natacha, Gonzalo Duarte-Clíments, Juan Gómez-Salgado, José Ángel Rodríguez-Gómez, and María Begoña Sánchez-Gómez. "Questionnaires Assessing Adolescents' Self-Concept, Self-Perception, Physical Activity and Lifestyle: A Systematic Review." Children 9, no. 1 (2022): 91.

[53] Kaziga, Ruth, Charles Muchunguzi, Dorcus Achen, and Susan Kools. "Beauty is skin deep; the self-perception of adolescents and young women in construction of body image within the Ankole society." International Journal of Environmental Research and Public Health 18, no. 15 (2021): 7840.

educate ourselves and gain awareness, identify the narratives we tell ourselves about who we are, and consider the integrity and source of those narratives to begin transforming our perception of ourselves. Do these concepts originate from our genuine experiences, societal categorizations, or anticipations, or do they reflect our true identities?

Once we identify and understand our self-perceptions, we will reshape them positively. This transformation is not about creating an unrealistic or inflated view of oneself but rather about cultivating a balanced, empowering perspective that recognizes one's abilities and potential for growth.

Ways to Transform Your Self-Perception

A proven approach for enhancing self-perception is the use of affirmations.[54] Affirmations are optimistic remarks expressed daily; they are repeated daily to strengthen useful self-perceptions. By consistently affirming "I am confident and can do anything," individuals may progressively transform their thinking from uncertainty to confidence. The affirmations must be tailored to the individual's ambitions and fundamental beliefs, ensuring they are unique and relevant.

Goal setting is another powerful tool. Setting clear, achievable goals provides a roadmap for action and growth. It enables people to demonstrate their skills to themselves via practical accomplishments. As objectives are achieved, the feeling of

---

[54] Mohebi, Laila, and Fatima Bailey. "Exploring Bem's Self Perception Theory in Educational Context." Encyclopaideia 24, no. 58 (2020): 1.

achievement reinforces a more favorable self-image, establishing a beneficial cycle of development and self-confidence.

Visualization techniques can also be beneficial. Through visualizing one's success in a particular endeavor, people could develop a more optimistic self-perception.[55] Visualization enhances self-assurance and primes the mind for the necessary activities to manifest accomplishment.

Finally, practicing self-compassion is vital. It takes time to change how one views oneself. It will take the same amount of kindness, encouragement, and persistence that you show towards your close relative or friend to motivate them. It will show your self-compassion, and it helps maintain a positive outlook on life regardless of failures.

How to break free from negative patterns?

Breaking free from bad habits is crucial for personal development and growth, especially for young people navigating the complexity of contemporary life. These ingrained tendencies, often due to prior encounters or learned actions, might prevent us from reaching our most significant potential.[56] Giving up on bad habits and developing a positive-change-promoting mentality are critical components of the transition from negative to positive practices.

---

[55] Kamhawy, Rana, Teresa M. Chan, and Shawn Mondoux. "Enabling positive practice improvement through data-driven feedback: A model for understanding how data and self-perception lead to practice change." Journal of Evaluation in Clinical Practice 27, no. 4 (2021): 917-925.
[56] Szostak, Michał, and Łukasz Sułkowski. "The identity and self-perception of artists-managers." (2021).

Strategies for forming new, positive habits

Recognizing and being aware of negative behaviors is the first step toward changing them. It's critical to recognize these patterns and comprehend what initiates them. Self-awareness may be developed by reflection, writing, or receiving feedback from reliable people.[57] To properly treat these behaviors, it is crucial to identify the situations or feelings that usually trigger them.

After negative patterns are found, it's critical to comprehend where they came from and why.[58] Negative habits are often coping strategies that formerly provided comfort or a way out of a stressful situation. Recognizing this may help one become more self-empathetic and facilitate transformation.

The next phase involves taking deliberate action to break these tendencies. This disruption may be accomplished by implementing new emotions or behaviors in response to recurrent stimuli. Suppose anxiety, for instance, causes you to avoid doing your regular tasks. In that case, you should take a little walk or engage in deep breathing exercises whenever the impulse to leave tasks in between arises. This is a transformation that takes time and constant work to achieve.

Strategies for forming new, positive habits are integral to this transition. One practical approach is to start small. Setting manageable, realistic goals makes these new habits more likely

---

[57] Crook, Ngaio, Ozan Nadir Alakavuklar, and Ralph Bathurst. "Leader,"know yourself": bringing back self-awareness, trust and feedback with a theory O perspective." Journal of Organizational Change Management 34, no. 2 (2021): 350-365.
[58] Bastick, Zach. "Would you notice if fake news changed your behavior? An experiment on the unconscious effects of disinformation." Computers in human behavior 116 (2021): 106633.

to be sustained. For instance, if the goal is to exercise more, commit to a few minutes each day rather than an hour-long session.

Moreover, one more way is habit stacking, which refers to pairing a new habit with an old one.[59] For example, if an individual has a routine of having coffee each morning, they may start composing a daily plan at that time. This correlation might facilitate the assimilation of the new habit easier.

The Power of Small, Consistent Actions

A widespread misunderstanding prevails that personal transformation involves making substantial and profound changes. However, it is a reality that the primary catalysts for significant and lasting transformation are little, consistent endeavors. Although these seemingly little daily activities and choices may seem unimportant, their combined effect may profoundly transform our lives.

The fundamental idea behind the impact of small actions is basic but profound: every significant accomplishment results from a series of little and constant efforts. For example, consistently writing a single page each day may result in completing a whole book within a year, while daily setting aside a small sum of money can gradually accumulate into a significant amount. These behaviors are effective because they are easily

---

[59] Tian, Xiaoyi, Zak Risha, Ishrat Ahmed, Arun Balajiee Lekshmi Narayanan, and Jacob Biehl. "Let's talk it out: A chatbot for effective study habit behavioral change." Proceedings of the ACM on Human-Computer Interaction 5, no. CSCW1 (2021): 1-32.

controllable; they do not need substantial bursts of exertion or drive, hence facilitating long-term commitment.

Resilience and persistence are essential in this entire process. Persistence refers to the capacity to continue progressing despite encountering obstacles and failures. The essence is in maintaining an unwavering dedication to your endeavors, regardless of their magnitude. Conversely, resilience is the ability to overcome unavoidable shortcomings and difficulties. It entails keeping a positive outlook and being open to changing and learning from mistakes rather than letting them depress you.

To maintain consistency in daily life, consider these actionable tips:

- **Set Clear, Achievable Goals:** Define your goals with your small actions. You must ensure that your goals are precise and realistic to keep you motivated and focused. [60]

- **Create a Routine:** Incorporate your small actions into your daily routine. Consistency is easier to maintain when your actions become as habitual.

- **Track Your Progress:** Record your daily actions and progress. This can be highly motivating and provides tangible proof of your commitment and growth.

- **Stay Flexible:** Be willing to adjust your actions if circumstances change. Flexibility is vital to maintaining long-term consistency.

---

[60] Janabergenova, A. J. "Setting Goals on Smart Techniques and Affecting Student Motivation." Annals of the Romanian Society for Cell Biology (2021): 9333-9336.

- **Focus on the Process:** Celebrate sticking to your routine, not just reaching your goal. This mindset shift helps maintain motivation, especially when progress seems slow.

These actions build momentum, gradually leading to significant changes that are sustainable in the long term. By practicing persistence and resilience and incorporating these actionable tips, anyone can harness the transformative power of small, daily actions in their journey toward personal growth and achievement.

Altering Others' Perceptions Through Our Actions

Our constant habits and activities over time, rather than a single action or statement, make us the way others see us. Redefining our perceptions of ourselves over time mostly depends on our consistent behavior, mainly when it aligns with our genuine beliefs and objectives. This process modifies our identity in the social setting subtly but very effectively.

The consistency of our behaviors conveys a distinct and cohesive statement of our identity and principles. For example, individuals who repeatedly exhibit kindness and compassion in their interactions would ultimately be acknowledged and valued for these attributes, even if they were not first seen as such. Likewise, demonstrating dedication to being on time and dependable in professional environments may change how others see you, shifting your image from unreliable to reliable and professional.

Nevertheless, this transition requires perseverance and a recognition that perceptions cannot be altered instantaneously.

Attempting to get instant approval for our activities might result in frustration and the possibility of abandoning the healthy habits we are trying to develop. It is crucial to bear in mind that change occurs gradually, particularly when it comes to perception. The long-term effects of our everyday actions are essential. Where we cannot see the impact immediately, but it becomes more substantial over time.

Though burdened with challenges, this journey holds the promise of transformation and growth, a testament to the strength in our daily actions. The power of consistency is not just a theoretical concept but a practical tool that can lead us to a life of fulfillment and purpose.

Remember, every incredible journey begins with a single step and then another. These small, consistent steps pave your path to a better life. Do not underestimate their power. They are the seeds from which the beautiful garden of your life will grow. Let this be your mantra: "Small steps, consistently taken, lead to significant change." Let it echo in your heart and mind as you face each new day. With each sunrise, remind yourself of your power to shape your destiny through your choices and actions.

We must have faith in the efficacy of consistency and persistently strive for the life we imagine. The journey may be extensive and even challenging, but the benefits of perseverance and unwavering dedication are invaluable. Your future self-will will be much appreciated, especially the devotion and commitment you provide now.

Proceed with the understanding that each little step has significance and every persistent endeavor carries weight.

Construct your life gradually, daily, with the steadfast conviction that a better existence is ahead. You have the freedom to go on your path, and it is up to you to fill the canvas of your life with the vivid colors of consistent hard work and unbeatable commitment.

Chapter 10: Seeing the Light

As we commence the concluding chapter of this book, it's crucial to reflect on the journey we have embraced together. This book was composed with a firm purpose: to empower you, the young adults standing at the crucial phase of life, to break the dilemma of perceived limitations, and to give your path a fulfilling and new meaning. Through the initial chapters, we delved deep into the roots of our beginnings and the generational cycles that often dictate our narratives.

Our journey through "Doomed From Birth" covered discovery, empowerment, and introspection. As we summarize the book, we must recognize the transformational arc we have followed, from understanding our origins to finding a path toward a self-defined future.

Our analysis began with acknowledging our roots—the inherited and societal cycles that mold our existence. Understanding our origins is not about blaming someone for anything wrong in our lives but recognizing patterns that may hold us back and rise from them. This awareness is the first step towards personal transformation, allowing us to break free from cycles that no longer serve us. By accepting our past, we gain the power to write a new chapter for ourselves and future generations. We then explored the critical steps of breaking free from these established cycles and the transformative power of our societal mindsets. Altering your mindset is about adjusting to new circumstances from a fixed perspective that sees limitations at every turn to a growth mindset that embraces opportunities and possibilities for change. This adjustment is essential, as it modifies our approach to life's challenges and our belief in our ability to overcome them. Our beliefs and thoughts significantly impact our emotions and reactions, and by learning to control our minds, we can take partial control of our destinies.

With a new mindset, we focused on the importance of outlining a plan that aligns with our latest purpose. Finding a purpose is similar to finding our focus in life—it gives us the direction to make decisions, fuels our motivation, and provides clarity in our chaotic lives. This practice offers a roadmap for identifying personal goals and crafting a plan to achieve them, stressing that purpose is about what we do and who we aspire to become.

The hunt for personal goals led us to self-discovery, a significant step in defining what we truly expect from life. This process of self-exploration is vital in understanding our deepest desires, strengths, and potential areas for growth. We also explored the essence of life's purpose, finding that it surpasses mere ambition, affecting the core of our being and what makes us feel most lively and fulfilled.

With a crafted plan and a deeper understanding of ourselves, we discussed the importance of adaptability, resilience, and unwavering commitment while facing unpredictable challenges. Being relentless is not about stubbornly shoving against all odds but about keeping a flexible yet determined mindset that keeps us moving ahead, even when life becomes uncertain.

Moreover, no path is tackled alone, and this book stresses the strength of the power and the vulnerability of seeking support. Asking for help reflects your strengths, not your weaknesses. It opens the door to new insights, perspectives, and the countless support of a community that can uplift and guide you through your darkest times.

Finally, we emphasized the profound impact of small, consistent actions. These choices and habits that we make in our daily lives gradually shape our reality, modifying how we see ourselves and how the world recognizes us. Consistency in our actions gives rise to confidence and manifests the transformation we wish to see in our lives.

As we reflect on these pivotal learnings, it's evident that the journey from being "Doomed From Birth" to watching the light of our built-in potential is paved with courage, self-awareness, and a persistent pursuit of growth. Each realization and step leads us closer to the life we desire to lead—a life defined by our difficult circumstances and responses to them.

Setting a Vision for Your Life

However, setting a clear vision for your life is as important as aligning a course for a ship in the vast ocean. Without an ultimate destination, you may find yourself drifting, subject to the impulse of the currents and winds. A vision gives purpose, direction, and a sense of transparency amid the fog of distractions and challenges in our daily lives. It serves as a guiding light leading you toward your desired future, illuminating the path through calm and turbulent phases. Understanding the keen importance of this vision is the initial step in transforming speculative dreams into tangible realities.

The journey from visualizing your ideal future to living it is connected by the diligent execution of a detailed plan. This plan is your roadmap, outlining the steps necessary to navigate from where you are now to where you wish to be. Meticulous work towards your vision is essential; the fuel moves the ship forward even against the heavy tides. No matter how small, each effort accumulates, setting the base for attaining your dreams. This process demands resilience, persistence, and a dedication to continuous adaptation and growth. Life's unpredictable nature means that plans may need adjustment, but with a clear vision, these changes become mere detours rather than roadblocks.

Additionally, creating strategies for setting accomplishable goals that align with your vision is critical. You should begin by breaking down your vision into manageable goals. These goals should be Specific, Measurable, Achievable, Relevant, and Time-bound (SMART). By making your goals specific, you clarify what success looks like. Then, measurability enables you to track growth, offering insight and motivation into adjustments that may be crucial. Now, you must ensure that your goals are achievable to keep them realistic and within reach, avoiding discouragement. Meanwhile, relevance ensures that each goal contributes directly to your comprehensive vision, maintaining efficiency and focus. Finally, assigning a timeframe to each goal creates a sense of urgency and helps prioritize tasks, making the vision more immediate and tangible.

Visualization techniques can enhance and strengthen your perception and objectives. Visualizing oneself attaining one's objectives not only enhances motivation but also aids in recognizing prospective challenges and associated solutions. Consistently reflecting on your goals and advancements strengthens dedication and enables essential adjustments.

Integrating feedback loops into your approach is an additional efficient strategy. Obtaining feedback from mentors and peers or engaging in self-reflection can offer invaluable perspectives, promoting personal development and knowledge acquisition. This feedback might illuminate overlooked opportunities or places for enhancement, honing your objectives and strategies.

Additionally, it is vital to recall significant achievements throughout the journey. Acknowledging and incentivizing oneself for the advancements achieved in pursuing one's objectives strengthens positive behavior and maintains progress. These celebrations remind you how far you have traveled and why you decided to undertake this adventure.

Essentially, establishing a vision for your life involves clearly and firmly declaring your ultimate goal. Engaging in meticulous planning, maintaining a consistent commitment, and strategically establishing attainable objectives are necessary to accomplish this vision. By adopting this methodology, you set a path toward a future where your aspirations and actuality align, demonstrating that with foresight and determination, the life you desire is attainable.

The Future Path

As we turn our eyes towards the future path, taking on the journey to realize our vision becomes a witness to our resolve and ambition. The initial steps towards this realization are crucial; they are the initial steps in a marathon of dedication and perseverance. This section aims to guide you through these steps, highlighting the importance of flexibility and underscoring the value of continuous growth, learning, and self-discovery.

Taking the Initial Steps

The journey commences with action. Procrastination and hesitation hinder progress. To get towards your envisioned outcome, begin by establishing modest and attainable objectives that serve as small steps towards your overarching aims. These preliminary measures should be practical and uncomplicated, alleviating the intimidating aspect of the present endeavor. Every action you take should aim to advance your vision, whether it involves enhancing talent, connecting with individuals who share your interests, or effectively managing your financial resources for future endeavors. Remember that embarking on a long and challenging journey requires taking the first step. Embrace the process and have faith that every step, regardless of its significance, contributes to the overall picture of your goal.

Flexibility and Adaptability

As you progress, you will inevitably encounter obstacles and challenges that test your resolve and force you to reevaluate your plans. It is here that flexibility and openness to adaptation become invaluable. The ability to pivot and adjust your strategies in the face of adversity is a hallmark of resilience and a critical aspect of realizing your vision. Life is unpredictable, and clinging too rigidly to a specific plan can lead to frustration and stagnation. Instead, embrace change as an opportunity for growth. Be willing to reassess and modify your goals and methods as necessary. This adaptability keeps you moving forward and enriches your journey with unexpected lessons and opportunities.

Continued Growth, Learning, and Self-Discovery

Achieving your vision entails more than simply attaining a series of objectives; it is a transformative expedition of self-development. The foundation of your aspirations rests upon the principles of perpetual growth, acquisition of knowledge, and personal exploration. Pursue continuous learning throughout your life, actively acquiring knowledge and skills that improve your capacity to accomplish your goals. This may entail developing knowledge through formal education, independent study, guidance from a mentor, or hands-on learning experiences. Every acquisition of knowledge and expertise enhances your capabilities and propels you closer to your objectives.

Furthermore, the journey is inherently a means of uncovering one's true nature. By confronting obstacles and celebrating achievements, you gain deeper insight into your capabilities, limitations, principles, and interests. The profound comprehension of yourself is of great worth, as it enlightens your choices and molds your future trajectory. Additionally, it enables you to synchronize your objectives more closely with your authentic identity, ensuring that the vision you pursue reflects your authentic essence and the person you aim to become.

Never Lose Faith in Yourself

As we reach the end of our journey, we must pause and reflect on the narrative we have unwrapped together. This book, your companion through moments of doubt and discovery, has sought to instill a profound truth within you: your ability to change your narrative is limitless, unbound by past or present circumstances. It's a testament to the resilience of the human spirit and a reminder that the pen that writes your life story is held firmly in your hands.

Belief in oneself is the bedrock upon which all success is built. It is the unseen power that drives us onward amid challenges, the quiet voice within us that reminds us of our potential when we are uncertain. This self-assurance extends beyond mere confidence in one's current capabilities; it encompasses having faith in one's capacity to acquire knowledge, develop, and overcome obstacles previously perceived as impossible to overcome. As you approach the future, remember that having confidence in yourself is the initial stride toward turning your aspirations into actuality.

As we close this book, I impart a final message filled with optimism and the ability to take control of your destiny. The upcoming stages of your existence are still to be determined, and the future is a space eagerly anticipating the realization of your ambitions. Remember that the world offers abundant opportunities for individuals who dare to envision and are resolute in pursuing those aspirations. Your envisioned future can materialize, and the challenges encountered are only opportunities for growth on the journey to achievement.

May this book serve as an enlightening guide during your journey and a constant reminder that even in the bleakest of times, the opportunity for a new beginning is never far away. Those who have faith in the allure of their aspirations and possess the bravery to pursue them actively will encounter a promising future. Have the courage to envision, dare to have faith, and have the courage to initiate that initial action. The world eagerly anticipates the unique contributions that only you can offer.